THE TURN OF THE TIDE

By H. M. Tomlinson

THE WIND IS RISING

and his novel

THE LIGHT OF MORNING

THE TURN OF THE TIDE

BY

H. M. TOMLINSON

NEW YORK

THE MACMILLAN COMPANY

1947

Contents

THE TURN OF THE TIDE

I

Log of a Voyage, 1935

OCTOBER 9. Our taxi-cab could do no more than short spurts, with long periods of tedium. But if our ship was to be found before she cast off we had no time to lose. I had another trifling anxiety, too. My son was my companion for this voyage, and our pursuit being a ship and the sea he would expect his father to get along better than this. Unlike the excitements of modern painting and poetry, the signs of the world's political hysteria shown in blaring newspaper headlines, and a few other matters of these latter days—which an elder man should not hope to understand—he would leave the first voyage we were making together to my longer experience and better knowledge. Where ships are concerned he would not dispute with me, though it is possible he suspects my acquaintance with maritime affairs is a long way astern of things as they are. If he does think so, he is right. I myself suspect my knowledge of the sea is well down the wake of the latest liner's cruiser-stern with turbines the drive. I do not reproach myself for this. I do not love modern drives.

Our cab was fixed in a jam of traffic near the Huskisson Dock. We must resign ourselves. Old Merseyside, in a steady autumn downpour, when you have no time to waste, will not be hurried. If you cannot get out and walk, stay where you are. It has seen many generations of eager travellers arrive and depart, and is sombre over its memories, and no wonder. We were stuck between glum warehouses and an adverse procession of lorries heavy with bales of raw cotton. When the cotton had gone we were caught by an eruption athwart us of wagons laden with barrels of apples. Cotton and apples have their own smells. The very odours vibrated and mingled in the thunder of wheels on a rough granite road. The antiquity of the walls just suited the eternal rain. We still waited.

But how good it was! Yes, it was good. This was life in the raw, elemental and impersonal. It heeded not the impatient hoots of our cabman. If we felt like hooting, we could hoot. But I can sit for hours and watch the flow of commerce moving slowly past me, amid the funnels and masts of docks; that is, I can when I myself am not outward bound on the turn of the tide. It was turning then, I guessed.

The road cleared, with the surprise of an unexpected gift of fortune, and we were within the dock. But that was all. A line of railway trucks went banging insultingly across our path. They were without beginning, and apparently without end. We might still do it, unless these freight cars were on an ever-flowing circuit. We were watching them pass, while hope passed too, when a coupling smashed, in answer to prayer, directly in front of us, and our driver shot through the risky gap. He pulled up at a shed; and there, he said, was our ship. All we could see was a section of the white superstructure of a liner. Her bulk lessened the importance of that part of Liverpool. My fellow-traveller is at least old and judicious enough to regret some aspects of these years of the modern. He is no longer awed, for example, by speed and magnitude, nor persuaded by the ubiquitous publicity for this and that, though his ears are still young enough to catch the low rumouring of the drums of a brave time not yet come. So he was not impressed by the size of this liner. He would have preferred, if I understood him rightly, a ship. Were we going to sea, he asked, or was this a pleasure cruise?

This liner, we presently discovered, was but our cab-man's mistake. The ship we were after had a name not unlike that of the big vessel, and sensible cabby had assumed, of course, that we were rational beings, and that when making a voyage we would continue along a deck that was a projection of a city's main thoroughfare, complete with tea-rooms, beauty-parlours, and cocktail-bars. A dock policeman overheard us and reached out an arm from a streaming waterproof. He pointed across the dock to another ship. There she was. There was the *Zircon* for us, as plain as rain and a late afternoon would allow.

My companion expressed his relief. That was the kind of ship he liked. I felt otherwise, but did not speak. I could not look upon the *Zircon's* trifling tonnage with full delight. This was mid-October, and when you have been across the Bay more than once, and see in a glance you must do it again in a vessel so small that she will be as emotional as a hen in a crisis, there is nothing to cheer over, nothing whatever. Indifference to pleasure-cruising may be a sign of manhood, but at my age to anticipate in joy the mixing of an Atlantic depression with a small steamer would be a sign of softening of the brain.

The only access to our ship's gangway was a ledge of granite quay, narrow and slippery, and cumbered with bollards and hawsers, running between the ship's side and a blank wall down which water-spouts were discharging. We were forced to take it—proof enough the *Zircon* cared nothing for passengers—because fore and aft of it were shed openings, cavernous and uncertain in the murk; and out of them, guided by electric flares high in the ship's rigging, goods were leaping continuously into the air, then descending into her holds amid shattering roars from steam-winches. What puzzled me was that Tommy exclaimed his delight when he saw a parcel of galvanized-iron buckets swaying aloft in a bluish glare, as splendid in the dark evening as a constellation. "That's the real thing," he said. "Why don't they paint that?"

Paint that, I thought? How is it to be done? For what is the real thing? Because I saw about us what Tommy did not, and could not; anyhow, not yet. Give him time. When that time comes, he may despair of painting it. Both his grandfathers knew this same apparition of reality, in the days of sail. Now we of today could smell wet straw, raw wood, and exhausted steam, and see the Blue Peter aloft. With it came a hot whiff from our ship's galley. The reality was harsh and uncomforting, and the splendour of iron buckets is of the hour and chance; but the scene was pleasantly peopled for me by shades who did not belong to it, yet who would have been at home there. Its smells and sounds were memorable of occasions long past, of voyages long since made. This energy of seafarers, and its certainty in the rain and dark, was of the tradition. I was at ease. But that was for me alone; so I was surprised, as well as pleased, to hear my fellow-traveller say, "This is good, isn't it?" Perhaps, then, he will paint it, or something like it, some day.

Our reception in the short alley-way leading to the *Zircon's* saloon was informal. We ran into her chief officer, and had to stop because he occupied its width. He was wearing a beret, and I fancied he was controlling mirth, when he learned we were voyaging with him. Across his working jacket was a row of grubby decorations won in war, among them one which is never given to a seaman for nothing. Despite his merry eye, which I supposed was for the comicality of fools, he had the bearing of a man to whom such an honour for doing well in battle would come by nature. He told us we had plenty of time; enough, he explained, to spend some in the town again, and suggested the advisability of going there and staying there. Why leave Liverpool? He still controlled his mirth. He merely inquired, "Have you *got* to come?"

No; but we would remain aboard, and if we failed to enjoy it we should still be there. The steward, a slight Cockney, with that look of sardonic tolerance and resignation so homely to another Londoner—and he too appeared to find that to wish to sail with him was a funny idea—led us to our cabin. It was an unusual cabin for a little ship. I have been much more meanly berthed in stately liners. It had three portlights; two opened forward, and one to starboard. What did it matter now that we did not know where we were going? All we knew was that she had many ports of call, and we were to see all of them. One, we knew, was Istanbul, famous once as Constantinople. But where and what is Ismir? We are said to be going there, and I had never heard of the place before, though an atlas is one of my favourite books, and the *Weekly Shipping List* used always to be at my right hand, an essential instrument of my work. Well, we did not know where we were going, and did not care; we were bound out. Then again, in the way of small jobs, is there one more attractive than unpacking gear and stowing it, at the beginning of a voyage? How else can be ascertained what necessary things have been left at home? This took us some while to sort out; and when we were free of it the sound of the winches forced itself on our attention again. Cargo was still going on.

We ventured out into, the dark, which was as wet as it was confusing. The ship poured with water. The night was disrupted by the lamps flooding light into the holds, and the rain glittered down. The cries of men, and the answering roars of engines, made the unseen corners of a strange deck still more dubious. The derricks and their impetuous loads swaying aloft appeared spectral and monstrous, giant limbs obedient to the signals of the uplifted hand of a man who gave no attention to peril overhead, but was peering into the ship's interior. This interval would have been dreary had this been a pleasure-cruise; but for us it had some compensation, though the beauty of kegs of paint, cases of soap, tin plates, motor-cars, and iron piping, swinging about dangerously, is not at once obvious. Yet it was a scene that has been native to our shores since coal and iron made all the difference to our country; and was usual long before that, for Tudor seamen must have known something of the sort, in a drizzle, at the beginning of winter. We were watching the job which does its best to keep us alive. Even agricultural tractors would come to a stand if what we were watching should ever languish, if the cause for this urgency failed at last to maintain flares over late cargo, and to keep stevedores busy when most people have done for the day. It is a scene known only to those who must be in it, and relished, I suppose, by fewer still. It is not worth a visit, and is without historical merit; it is unknown to artists, and never prompts a song. Once, alone at night, I sat by an old shipman while he was dying. He was lost already to this world. I looked at his stern countenance, grey-bearded, and his white hair tumbled on his pillow, and wondered just where he was then; not here, and not yet there. While I watched him, knowing that he was now finished with me, he opened his eyes to the ceiling, and lifted his right arm magisterially from the counter-pane, as though to order a matter; then lowered it gradually, as if steadying something in descent. His open hand paused, and then, suddenly, fell flat on the bed. It was finished. I sup-pose he had been by the coaming of a hatch, of a ship that made her last voyage years ago. I know that whatever that man did in life was just. I think his final instinctive gesture would have been accepted.

That motor-car was the last of the cargo for the *Zircon*. She fell silent. So did the quay. The men began to put on her hatch covers, and as if in a hurry to be off. We returned to our cabin. Later, it was noticed that cold air was pouring down a ventilator, so we plugged it. Better stuffiness than a flood of frozen ozone, if you want to sleep.

October 10. The next morning was fresh, and it sparkled. Our course was south 35 west, into the weather. Only the Irish Sea was in sight. Men in tarpaulins were clearing the deck. The seas were on the starboard bow, and increasing. She was not down to her mark by three feet, owing to more threats of war, and her head was giddy, lifting and falling to showers of spray. It was impossible to get about without a soaking. We were assured this was all to the good, and that we should be glad of it, because when she is full she is treated as disrespect-fully as a half-tide rock. The steward—we found later that he was one of the best seamen aboard—remarked that she was "a clumsy old bitch and ought to be scrapped." In heavy weather, he went on, men sleeping aft had to crawl along derrick booms over the deck, but often couldn't make it, and slept in the saloon. The steward did not look at me when speaking. He was too tired. He addressed himself to Tommy. Perhaps he thought the younger man, who smiles when unhappy difficulties are named, would be more sympathetic through a better under-standing of the world as it is. Elder men, of course, think they are wiser about things that are to come, but the young cer-tainly have sounder knowledge of things present, and so are more dependable.

We were abreast the Smalls, the lighthouse at the entrance

to the Bristol Channel, in the late afternoon. The sunset was bright and hard. It was bleak on the oilskins of the men, and turned the black hatch tarpaulins into polished brass as she rolled. The spray came over her, in the level light, as sheets of fiery hail. My companion clung to the dodger and was enjoying it.

"Look!" he cried. A mile to port a schooner was dim within the curtain of a cloud, but in tacking a beam found her, and she was radiant in an instant. She became more glorious than a ship ever is. As she heeled she flashed, as if giving out fire. She was signalling eternal renown to us.

"There's *Argo* for you," I jollied him.

Tommy laughed. "What an idea!" he said. "Well, so she is, for us."

"But don't try to paint it."

"Why not?"

"Who would believe it, if you did?"

"There she is. We see her."

"In a way, we see her. There's the old old story for us, the ship that cannot founder, in a day of the past. But who but ourselves ever believes the shining image seen in the one moment when we are above all doubt?"

He did not answer. He still eyed her. This, I could see, was puzzling. That schooner was certainly a splendid aspect of reality, as if for a moment illumination had come, and the truth of existence were glimpsed. There we saw revealed the ultimate honour of drudgery in the dark, where travail is uncertain of purpose. She was transfigured, that ship. She was the image of the original ship in an unnamed sea when men dared the unknown for the first time to find what God had hidden. She was that. But she was also untrue, for she did not accord with some facts as we know them. If she were painted as we saw her, her own men would deride the representation. So to suggest her to be as noble as a burst of music superior to time and space would be only a lie, after all? Tommy admitted this was so, regretfully.

"Only the Heroes would know her," I suggested.

His reply was a gesture of impatience. She was another illusion, like the cluster of galvanized-iron buckets we had seen oscillating over a hatchway, in the glare of a spot-light.

Yet how are we to distinguish illusion from reality? It is possible that matter and spirit are not two, but one. That idea should not confuse us still more. It ought to make the earth and our existence upon it less of a mystery. If matter is alive, being informed by spirit, then illusion need not be deception. Reality is versatile. I have heard of an airman, his flying machine out of hand in the vortex of a storm-cloud, catching sight of a thermos-flask floating above his head like a bubble. Astonished, he grabbed it, and found himself clinging to it, his sole support, with his feet off the floor; and though he still deeply respects a force called gravitation, he wonders now, with Einstein, whether that force is all that old-fashioned physicists, following Newton, supposed it to be. Tommy was right in his insistence on facts, and no nonsense about them. But the worst kind of disastrous nonsense can be made of facts alone. So of what good is art, if it does not give us with the thrill of appearance an impression of continuity in time without end?

"How I wish," he exclaimed, "I could get such a light on common shapes!"

"That's the thing to do. Keep at it. Never give up. Light is the thing to give them."

He smiled. I have seen that smile before. Trust these old 'uns, it means, who lost their dreams in their old war, to hold

on desperately to one tiny feather of mysticism, as a souvenir.
They will stick to their last scrap of Plato if the heavens fall.
I was aware of his reservation. Better leave the old people
alone! They cannot help it. Young men thus regard their
elders, who have made a pretty mess of affairs, with the silent
reproach they deserve. Not always silent either. The mistakes
and worse of their teachers and leaders have brought about an
anarchic world, in which they must build anew, if they can
find the material for it, but with no principles to go upon that
they have not learned to distrust. Nothing appears to be left to
them for guidance save self-interest; and that puts them back
at the beginning, before temples appeared, when everybody
lived in caves. There is no common bond for youth, unless it be
found in a preposterous uniform, with a pagan symbol. Faith
has come down to knuckle-dusters.

Then how is reconciliation to come about? And reconciliation there must be, if civility is to endure, and growth continue.
Unless such as Tommy and I can agree about first things, then
out of the conflict between past and present the future will be
to Caliban's progeny. I could find no clue to it, no clue that a
young intellectual would accept with gladness, while waiting
in my bunk that night for sleep. I was only sure that the sea
was keeping to its old ways. No change was there. The sea was
in a rough mood. I did not disapprove. I sank with our ship as
she dived into a trough. The up-ended screw shook her ribs.
Now she was going to catch it! Then waters crashed on the
forward bulkhead of our cabin. Cataracts poured loudly
through the gear outside. But by her buoyancy and rhythm it
was certain that, though she was a clumsy old bitch, as the
steward had warned us, she knew her work. She was used to it,
this little thing. Here was the hard and simple life, as Tommy
admired it, with no frills. Any man of that ship's crew, I could

guess, would accept joyfully the first good job ashore he was offered; at that moment, anyhow, he was swearing that he would. So how was my cabin-mate relishing the primordial sea which knows no change, but goes on still as it did when day was first made separate from night? He answered that he was cold.

There again I saw a difference between us. Though we were in the same ship, the two of us must make separate voyages with varying experiences. We should share the same daylight, see the same landfalls at the same time, yet reality for each of us would be anything you like to name. The sea, ancient and changeless, could not reconcile us with its hint of continuity, the same yesterday, today, and for ever.

October 12. I saw evidence that we were in worlds apart after we found ease in our encounters with the men of the ship. Tommy they accepted straight away, as one of themselves, worthy of dry asides, fit to take the rough retort. They recognize their own kind, and that is good. They are polite to me. I am not of their year. He merged with the ship's company before we could find our way at night about the deck. During the morning watch, there he was on the bridge, in affable converse with the ship's chief officer. I don't suppose Tommy had so much as noticed that sailor's signal war-decoration, and I am quite sure the sailor had forgotten he was wearing it. It was grubby. There the pair of them were, however, as if they had known each other for years, happy on the windward side of the bridge over a joke not for my ears.

Our first port of call, I hear, will be Casablanca. As for me, alone on the lee side, I felt I would not protest very much if we returned from there. I am fortunate enough. I am on more than one voyage, and have shipmates not on this ship's articles.

Phantoms are about. My companion doesn't know that. The smells have called them up; they idle along where the sunlight is of another year, though it is lively still in the familiar white of an alley-way. A film of water quivers on the hatch covers, as if it had not dried since first I saw it like that, but had remained quick and sensitive. The wind is shrill in the gear, singing the old tune. The moist air has a taste of iron.

As I meditated, Tommy came across to tell me that we are to coal at Algiers when returning. He is pleased. He wants to see Algiers. Of course he does. His desire must be hereditary. I praised it once to the Chief of a ship then on her way to the Amazon. He confessed it was a favourite port with him, too, and sighed. He called there on his first voyage. He was sentimental. He then remarked regretfully, "We shan't see Algiers this trip, not by a damned long way." Twenty years later I was by his side when he was barely conscious and was rambling. He began to mutter, and I bent over him to listen. This might be important. He was saying, "We shan't see Algiers this trip, not by a damned long way." Yes, he was saying that. I tell that story here, but I did not then tell it to Tommy. We both dodged a flight of spray instead. A Russian steamer, much more up to date than our own, had overtaken us, and was crossing our bows. She was flying the Hammer and Sickle.

The truth is that, apart from sentimental retrospection, this *Zircon* and her men make so extraordinary a muddle of past and present that I am already aware this latest voyage of mine is my first, in a way of speaking, and I haven't got used to it yet. Her master and his lieutenant were in the war. Their apprentice years were spent under sail. They speak familiarly at table of historic clippers and famous runs, but I fancy their juniors must wonder what it all means, though aware those great days were not so very long ago. The gulf between youth

and maturity is made not by time but by a revolution. The
younger officers are public school and Conway boys. Square-
rig to them, and the Great War, have joined Drake and Trafalgar. I think the difference is even deeper than that. It is a
clean break from the past, with forgetfulness. The tradition of
the elder men I know, but I do not know the gods of the
younger seamen. Sparks quotes Lenin at meals; that is all I
can tell you. One day the three of us at the head of the table
were a trifle loud with each other over Jutland, and Jellicoe
and Beatty. The juniors below, I suddenly noticed, looked as if
they would have been happier with a bright discussion on
vacuum-cleaners. They are mathematicians and scientists. They
condemn our ships' reciprocators for not being turbine or
motor. The clipper ship to them is that dusty model in grand-
father's study. Jutland is only a name.

There is something else. I was passing a cabin the first night
out, and was stopped, was almost shocked, by a rich and languorous contralto voice confidential within. Why, but that was
the cabin of a young engineer! However, it was all right. The
lady herself was in Paris or Rome, or somewhere. Again, this
evening, a lee bunker-hatch being dry at last, I was sitting
there cutting up a stick of tobacco. The moon was rising.
Tommy came along, gazed into the distance for a minute, and
then sat beside me. "Japan is threatening us," he remarked.

"What's that?"

"I said Tokyo is breathing fire and slaughter."

"What do you mean? Who said so?"

"Don't know his name—the news has just come through."

So that was it. I had forgotten every cabin in a ship may
now have an ear open to the ebullience of the round globe. I
found later that the *Zircon* has seven radio sets. One is in the
forecastle. Tommy amplified his information. Germany was

still shouting haughtily at Europe. Mussolini had added more words of threatening insolence to the air. There had been floods in the Midlands; and our ship's company even then was sharing the football pool. They get the football results from London almost as soon as the games are over. While I had been at peace on a bunker-hatch, hearing only the sough of the seas at dusk, other men were picking up those various glad tidings from overhead.

Tommy strolled away. He showed no surprise at a marvel which allows a ship lifting strange stars to know as much, or as little, as the people who are snatching at evening papers to read on their way home from Victoria station. Once upon a time you could be apart from the disturbance and distraction of cities. When departure was made and the last English head-land had sunk astern, you fell back on your centre. You might hear from yourself at last, and recognize a private thought, with luck. Never again. Solitude is abolished. It seems we ought to be grateful for this, but I say there are as many senti-mental rose-buds presented as thank-offerings for the marvels of science as were ever given to Cupid. Some useful research work might be done to discover to what extent our practical cleverness has deprived us of benefits of greater value than it has added to the technology of the mechanical arts. This, I know, is the new blasphemy, but now and then that shocking doubt must be expressed for relief. Even the master of this ship is on a length of string, and an office-boy in the owner's office often pulls it, to let him feel the brevity of his liberty. I had been startled, like a fool, by some of the eager talk at our mess-table which had sounded like the headlines of a sensational newspaper. The talk in a ship used to be intimate and within her bulwarks. Now I understand. We shall never be free again, never be at large any more, never look up undistracted to the stars.

Well, the sea is as ever, and there in the east the same old moon is looking at us, a face of primrose with clouds of pearl and rose madder about her, the one the earliest seamen watched when they ventured through the forbidding Pillars, and boldly turned north. For all that, our *Zircon* is not only in another age, but another world; and here I am, making my first voyage in it, with all to learn. I am a beginner again. I must keep an eye on particulars, if old impressions and past experience are not to mislead me. These common smells of a cargo ship, her movements, the sounds of winds and waters, the casual friendliness of shipmates, have an odd effect on an old voyager, off again after a long spell ashore. He feels he has floated away into a dimension where time is never counted, and nothing new can happen. What he hears are echoes in the hollow of eternity. He could easily believe he is continuing a long voyage begun in a year he has forgotten. On the bridge at midnight the bell on the ship's head answers the bridge, while the dim foremast head rakes the stars; and then the shadows arrive which are the relief for the middle watch. He knows those shadows. They always appear at this hour. He suspects they are never seen by daylight. "South 30 West it is, sir!" That grave voice of the unseen fellow who has just taken the wheel was known, doubtless, in the night that is now antiquity.

If I must we wary lest these signs of a tradition as old as history deceive me, because men's opinions of late have gone widdershins—which augurs, if it augurs anything, a tempest of conflicting doctrines—why should I expect Tommy and his generation to give attention to old values and virtues? Are they applicable, in this latest dangerous phase of man's vivacity? For, despite the admonitions of the saints, sages, and prophets, from Zoroaster to Jesus and his disciples, it appears today as if there were but one good we all should respect, whether we want to or not: we must bow to the political use of power

directed to full control of the lives of our fellows. The last aim
of reason, therefore, is to refuse to human life the use of reason;
so down we go to the uniformity of sheep. But will we go down?
There is sure to be trouble about that. The individual soul for
ever, in London, and Pekin, and every Kaffir kraal, against
all the assumptions of outside authority!

Just as I was about to turn in I met Dicky, our chief officer.
Already I know him well enough to say that fear would be
taken out of calamity at sea if you saw that man tackling it. It
appears he had verified our position by the stars, and I was
glad to hear it. He knows just where we are. He has consulted
Altair and Jupiter. Jupiter, no less! "Time we did get our
whereabouts from him," I said to Dicky. He paused, gave me
a nudge, and laughed.

October 13. This ship has plenty of top hamper amidships
and aft. You cannot promenade. You must dodge about. In a
few steps you are brought up by a winch, a hatch, or a rail, or
go overside. There is the foredeck, but only an acrobat could
manage its sheer when a sea is up. The wind follows us today,
what there is of it, but a moderate swell runs from west. We
are well across the Bay. While we were peering from the rails
of the forecastle head into the vitreous send of the waters,
Tommy retailed a few facts of life afloat. The men talk freely
to him. He has been given the entry, which I shall not get, into
the smells and damp of that forbidden and forbidding sanctuary, the forecastle. Nineteen men sleep there, and he doubts
that he could. They have one privy between them, one wash-
house, and no bath. One of the fellows told him that his head
hit a beam over his bunk four times while she was pitching.
The idea that seamen are jolly savages, and don't care, has a
profit motive, and so will take long to die. "The honour and

glory of the merchant service?" gaily exclaimed an officer here to me; "you'd say so, if you'd peddled scrubbing-brushes from door to door after the war was over, with your extra-master's ticket in your pocket to prove to suspicious women you were not after the spoons. Mister, we were left on the pavement when our country didn't want us on navigation bridges and gun-platforms. Next time, if there is another war, me for the Church."

It was warm in the sun when we gathered for boat drill. I see I shall be all right in my boat with the crew of toughs told off for it, bare-footed, nonchalant, unshaved, their chests and arms elaborately tatooed in blue and red. This tatooing by seamen was for use, I guess, in its origin, and not for ornament. It was not barbaric. With known marks on you, if washed ashore you had a better chance of Christian burial.

The drill over, the captain eyed a large Italian steamer to starboard, steering north. She was empty. It pleased him to note that "sanctions" imposed by the League of Nations as a deterrent to Italy's war on Abyssinia, though partial, have had some effect. He asked, however, whether Mussolini's sub-marines would be out before he could touch Malta. That indeed may happen. Looking round, though, at sunset, war seemed not only monstrous but impossible. A few small amber clouds were scattered, the isles of the blest, high in a vault of gold. Distant ships were black shapes on a hard horizon, a lucent wall beyond them. The Asturian mountains lifted as a purple immensity, a storm nimbus, in the south-east. The moon rose into a clear sky, with the glims of fishing craft hovering a mile away; and there was no sound but the hypnotic monody of our wake. On the port bow is Finisterre, that august landfall, the shape of a black whale with a diamond flashing in its head. Between that cape and a more eastern point, Cape

Ortegal, is the town of Corunna. The long Atlantic seaboard of Iberia is haunted to all seafarers; it is grave with memories for the English.

Tommy was gazing at the famous headland. He would not remember, and I did not remind him, that not a drum was heard, not a funeral note. . . . I was going to do it, but saw it was foolish. Young people must be weary of that aspect of history. Let the dead past bury its dead. Yet the trouble with the past is that it is not dead, not all of it, not much of it. Does it ever die? It must rule us in a way we barely surmise. The very dust of it is organic, and we never know what we may release when we disturb it. It may have in it the light we need, or the beginnings of earthquake and eclipse. All history walks alive in our own day. Whatever the relics of prehistory and the sands of Egypt may be keeping from our knowledge, we have it in our bones.

The names of landmarks on this coast, bound south as we are, remind a traveller, especially an English traveller, that the high dark mass to port has witnessed its fair share of the great events which set men cheering, and then, not long after, filled them with foreboding. We are watchful this very night through foreboding. The dust of history is stirring in Europe. We hear the sullen mutterings of many peoples, sometimes increasing to a challenge to God knows what, hear it all even in this ship, though the night about us is like everlasting peace.

I was admiring the profile of Dicky in a good light at sunset, his cap pushed back. He was bent over the desk in the chart-room. He was larky, and hummed a tune. If the illustrious names on the chart under his nose meant anything to him, except the ship's course, he did not say so. But what of that? The headlands here will not forget him and his kind. He and they have been up and down this coast for many centuries, and have left their mark. You might think Dicky merely a kindly man, stocky, prudent, and deliberate. His light-hearted speech could hint that he was more prone to dodge a difficulty than to face it. I am certain no foreigner would ever read him for what he is, and thereupon show him the respect of a careful approach. Dicky is an English sailor. He has helped to beat a ship to windward round Cape Horn so often that his gay reminiscences of tribulation are both easy and outrageous. He commanded a Q ship, a Cornish topsail schooner, "with a coffee-grinder in her stern," in the war, fought two submarines in an afternoon, sinking one and filling the other with fear, though his armament was inferior; but his yarn of the encounter is as informal as the tactics of Cochrane, yet equally on the target, and told with something of the sly innocence of Artemus Ward. He is a dangerous man, with a friendly regard, and audacious with his cunning where there is hostility, and you might never guess it.

I stood beside him, reading the chart. I love the quiet of a navigating-room, with its sight of the ship's head. Once in the North Atlantic, after a week and more of weather that all but sent us under, and seemed heavy enough to have swept the ocean of anything afloat, the captain looked out from his chart-room, and exclaimed. I could see nothing beyond us but elemental rage. The seas were daunting, though the wind had lessened and the sky had risen to allow more light and a deeper prospect. He pointed. There she went, a small steamer, labouring, heading into it, and expunged alarmingly at times by intervening ridges; she was the first sign to us, after our time with a hurricane, that life went on. She hoisted the Red Ensign. One of ours, that ship. There she went. You would have cheered, had you seen her.

Dicky was relating an amusing story of Oporto. Ahead of

us the Douro comes to the sea. South again, the lines that Wellington built, against which Napoleon's army in Iberia was broken, touch the coast by Torres Vedras. We shall be off the Tagus tomorrow, from which Philip's Armada set forth. Cape St. Vincent is beyond, and round the corner is Cadiz, Cape Trafalgar, and Gibraltar. It is natural for an English voyager to be thoughtful in these waters. "Here and here did England help me: how can I help England?" Could I quote Browning to Dicky? How he would have laughed! But he is of the very men who long ago stood to their guns off these promontories of Portugal and Spain. He never thinks of that, and would make fun of the idea. He himself refers to war as preposterous imbecility, which spoils everything, and out of which you are lucky if you can get as much as a laugh. But it would be no laughing matter to upset him.

October 14. The steward woke us. Does that man never rest? It was scarcely daylight; but he said the chief officer wanted us on the bridge. Some more of Dicky's nonsense? Up we mounted and before the sun, though he was not far off. Straight over the ship's bows was the imposing south-west corner of Europe, the Promontorium Sacrum of the ancients, Cape St. Vincent. Our steamer closed it. Portugal of the past, of Henry the Navigator, might have been illustrious with unfading renown in the pallor of dawn; anyhow, there was a margin of bright gold to the high ridge of that country. Then the sun peeped over the top of it, though we lost him again as we drew within the cold shadow of the foreland; drew close enough to stare straight up, and wonder why those steep inclines, dimly green, did not slip into the night of the lower chasms, where nothing could be seen but seas shouldering between the buttresses and thundering up from inner darkness as white smoke. Another steamer was ahead of us. She cleared the over-shadowing promontory and entered morning light as she rounded for Trafalgar. She was so exalted on the instant that her underwriters would have believed she was immortal. Crowning the cape is a lighthouse tower, and a white convent building is beside it, holding up the Cross over the Western Ocean. As we in our turn cleared the point, our ship, and the eastern honey-coloured coast diminishing towards Cadiz Bay, were in immediate day. What an earth is ours, if only we knew how to make the right use of it!

We stood on for Casablanca, and arrived somewhere near it in a fog next morning. We could not see our forecastle, but could feel the shuddering of our melancholy siren, which had only echoes for answer. On an off-shore wind there was a smell of aromatic herbs. The fog cleared, and tawny slopes grew out of it with white cubes of houses dotted about them. It was Tommy's first experience of Africa. For a brief while he saw it as it was for Tudor seamen; but we entered the port, and made fast at a quay—a new concrete quay. Then we might have been in France; and the French, as civil engineers, could improve Utopia into Detroit. The harbour and its works of steel and concrete were daunting in extent, and paralysing with efficiency. The geometrical appearance of Africa shocked Tommy. We made our humble way across the hot and dazzling desert of concrete and railway metals into the town. There we sat outside a brand-new café at a metal table under the sprinkled shade of a youthful mimosa. We had a good view of new flats across the road. Those flats might have been any-where, from the Marylebone Road to Montevideo. Tommy expressed his sorrow. Call this Africa!

"It used to be," I assured him. "It was when I saw it first."

"What, this place?"

"This place. It was only a mosque and an Arab town. It had nothing but goats, agriculture, a citadel, ophthalmia, and the Koran."

"It has a lot more now. It must surprise the Moors."

"It surprises us."

"Anyhow, ophthalmia has been civilized out of it."

"Has it? We'll go along to the old quarter. You shall see for yourself, if you think you can face it."

"Here, just look at these local newspapers! Would you believe it? The French here are dead against the Spanish Republic. They talk like Fascists."

"Of course they do. They've a native population swarming about them, they're rather afraid of it, and Fascism gives fearful but truculent simpletons, at this late hour, a return of the confidence they were losing in the tide of events. It won't last."

"It won't? But suppose it does, what shall we do?"

"I don't know. Flit somewhere, if there's a place left on earth. What about Patagonia?"

But the sun was pleasant, and the wine. A girl passed us in a smart victoria, with a coachman and an elegant grey horse. She was lounging. Her riotous hair was a brassy green, and she wore a canary-coloured jumper, corduroy breeches, brown riding-boots, and her mouth was as evident as a dab of red sealing-wax on blank parchment. Two of our firemen were sitting with us, for they had been passing, and appeared lost. One gazed at the retreating carriage, and then at me, as if to confirm that he was quite all right and had not been deceived.

We idled away to the market in the old town. Engineering can flourish where noisome hovels rot to a degree that would poison the body of any community; and at the same time aerial wires link up a common opinion everywhere in these native slums. Next to an apothecary's shop—the black-bearded

medicine-man wore a white turban—with dried cat-skins for
sale and the mummied heads of sea-birds, hawks, and crows,
desiccated lizards, and amulets, and other things to show an
undying faith in magic, was a coffee-shop. In it, about a
brazier, a group of natives were listening, heads solemnly bent,
to what was issuing from a radio box. Tommy by now had seen
all he wanted of ophthalmia as well as the symptoms of worse
afflictions. It is possible the spread of Fascism itself is but an
outcome of febrile morbidity, desperation induced by hopelessness. I do not know what thoughts occur to these Jews, Berbers,
Arabs, Negroes, poor whites, and half-castes, a congested multitude in a prolific squalor, but if fermentation of the head exists
with them, and I hear it does, then the radio and the cinema
may do the rest. Our science does not appear able to regulate
the wilderness of the mind as easily as it defines the spaces of
earth with railway tracks and air routes.

October 16. I have often seen the Rock from a deck, but
have thought that was near enough. Once when at Algeciras I
was invited over, but interest was too weak to move me. We
are at Gibraltar today, and it is good. We climbed to the
Moorish castle up streets that were stairways, broad below, but
narrowing in winding ascent. Women leaned out of meridian
windows and lowered market baskets on cords to street vendors
whose vegetables were loaded on mules in the depths. Those
housewives needed pulleys, at that height. Canaries in cages
were sprinkled about sunny walls, singing away. In one shop,
projecting as a low oriel from a tower, where we paused for
breath, was a jar full of coloured glass marbles, the first I have
seen since a boy, and we bought a double handful for luck.

The castle kept us. We were alone in it. Its openings had
varied releases from caverns across the bright bay and over

the ships to Spain. Its walls were scored with graffiti. The scratchings went back through the years to 1789, with the names of British soldiers of the Great Siege. Its shadowy galleries and recesses did their silent best to relate what they remembered of the centuries, but, though eager to hear, we found that the loud events of yesterday and the present had dulled our understanding. We felt we were but partially aware of admonitions all about us; and that awareness, touched with some concern, is a very proper mood in which to attempt to read history, for one then knows at least the easy possibility of error in reading the news of the day, through haziness of causes and origins. An idea came over me in Gibraltar that, to be on the safe side, I would rather the leaders and provocative agents of the revolt against reason everywhere in Europe were all cast down, even as low as utter damnation, than that our flag should be lowered at the Rock. Some day it may come down, but this is not the day.

What we learned at Casablanca was disturbing. That Frenchmen should look on the Spanish Republicans as enemies, but see good in Mussolini's Rome, was not a little alarming to the innocence and ignorance of English admirers of Anatole France. I pay homage to the French, while doubting they will ever believe that to very many Anglo-Saxons their country is not only comely and comfortable, but as important as home. Anglo-Saxons I know are amusing dunces, for we have been told that often enough; we are without the fine discrimination in the things of the spirit that is the specialty of intellectual Latins. Some of these Latins, especially in London, are Latin only by adoption, or anticipation, for they are, or will soon become, Roman Catholics. A puzzling change will sometimes take a man when he is persuaded and goes over. Then he sees all from one side only; no other side exists, except as a mirage reflected from the Reformation. He sees too, for the first time, that his own people are not Latins, far from it, but are bony-headed, and at their worst are loutish, the poor victims of northern clay and fog, beef and pudding, the English Channel, and Puritanism. They will never know why they are being laughed at. No Briton, still unadopted as a Latin, can be quick enough in the intellects to gather that he is a figure of fun, nor see why so often he rouses indignation which is righteous. Of course, he cannot help it; that is fairly recognized. His grandparents knew no better than to admire George Eliot as a poet, and look to Ruskin as a prophet. So what would you expect?

Still, while aware I dare not claim relationship with the lucent south, where truth is clear, at the same time I was never able to chant with Kipling, and with the best of British patriots, the glories of our blood and state; not without slight embarrassment; not without a nervous desire to turn round to see who was looking on with a faint smile. Long ago, in the days of the Boer War, I was advised that the only cure for my malady was a lamp-post; and since nobody took the trouble to run me up then, I have grown worse, and not better. For this very reason, the best I can offer, it seems to me that Rome and Berlin are hastily calling up the legions of the pit to destroy all that has made human endeavour in the past worth one's own trifling effort in the preservation of proved values. And if the French will not stand by us in that, where are we?

You could not help remarking that the spacious quays and port machinery of Casablanca, where the Cross has conquered the Crescent on a desert shore, make the older docks of Liverpool seem casual and slovenly. In North Africa it is plain there are Great Powers, of remarkable enterprise, and jealous of their exclusive privileges, who will not deal with Morocco,

Algeria, Tunis, and Tripoli, as will the British with Egypt and India. Is it because the British have attained, through much tribulation, a more enlightened outlook on human relationships in industrial civilization, that Herr Hitler and Signor Mussolini, and many Frenchmen too, think that we are now on the soft side? If Italy occupied Egypt, we can guess how much self-government Black Shirts would allow to Cairo. Mussolini cannot see that we are fumbling with a better idea, but supposes we are merely tired under the White Man's burden. Tolerance, an attempt to find out how the other fellow keeps going, he no more wants to understand than a criminal would study to understand the law, except to avoid it. If you are well disposed it stands to reason you must be weak in the head; a simple error, frequently made by lusty men, as well as by the wits of the day.

It was that conviction, I imagine, which gave Mussolini, just before our ship's arrival at the Rock, the assurance to broadcast news of a coming Roman conquest of Gibraltar, Malta, and Egypt. He thoroughly frightened the natives. They began to watch for his war-planes. They looked round anxiously to see whether British policemen were still present. They too may have been Fascists, of a kind, liable to excitability, as occasion offered, through a hearty go at grandiloquence, and in such hours worried their administrators. But when Mussolini promised them "a splendid display of force" they began to feel they could get along just as well without it. There was more comfort in the routine of the local post-offices. When we moored at Gibraltar, that broadcast had already brought troops and warships down south. Those battleships, for once in a way, comforted people who till then had been in the habit of looking on the White Ensign as the token of abiding tyranny. Gibraltar, the day we arrived, had ceased to expect the Italian fleet with

was invisible, because two thin gleams of light stole out from the men's quarters, and held the eye. The look-out man was with us on the bridge, unable to stand on the delirious forecastle deck, with the wind in his face. Dicky was worried about fishing-boats. They were likely to be on our course, and either they carry no lights, or show feeble and misleading lanterns. Those interfering gleams from the forecastle were ordered to be shut off. I then saw, or thought I did, faint intermittent glittering dead before us, though miles away; but while I was making up my mind about it Dicky ported the helm two points to clear it, and a cluster of fishing boats, and men shouting, swept close alongside in a matter of seconds. I think a life of watch-keeping at sea must develop a special sense. The clamour of the seas and wind, the pitching and rolling of the ship, and the night so dark you could not see your handhold, persuaded me that fishers might have perished had I been in charge.

I stayed topside till the half-moon was sitting on the summit of a black lump of nimbus, under which lightning was shimmering incessantly, and then went below to read. Even guidebooks give out more meaning in the seclusion of a ship's cabin, at night; and if you are in the Mediterranean, then, despite present noises, the plunging of water on the bulkhead, the telling of the watches, and the sudden uproar when someone —who ought to know better—opens the alley-way door on the windward side, you feel your own night is coeval with all the ages. There are undertones. The bells which warn of another hour past have a note of irony. On the shores around this sea we began; all of us. Twenty thousand years ago! Hereabouts the first metals were chanced on, and the first ships built. In a ship's middle watch, the echoes from the dark backward of Egypt, Palestine, Athens, and Rome, turn the immediate boisterous night without into the same importance as the news the

steward whispered glumly from the latest broadcast, when he
brought in a drink for me, and one for himself, and sat down
on the edge of my bunk to yarn for ten minutes. I've learned
a lot from that steward, including some things I ought not to
know. Yet, remembering where I am, it should not surprise me
that Pan is not dead. His bearded lips still rise at the corners
when he smiles. He does not smile like the scholars. Our steward is but the latest footnote in the interpretation of the legends
of the prime. I am of a mind to take any myth, any improbable yarn, in this cabin, after the middle watch, midnight, is
set. The more improbable it is, then the likelier. Could it be
more fantastic, harder to believe, than what men are saying
and doing at this hour along these shores?

October 18. We were out of sight of land this morning till
we lifted the coast of Algeria. The sun is comforting, and the
sea quiet. The coast grew plainer, till houses came out on the
tawny slopes, and mountains beyond with slow storms of rain
dissolving their summits one by one. The rigging and gear are
unusual with many birds, finches, black-caps and other war-
blers, a thrush in a cross-tree, and several robins. One robin did
not bother about us. He must have met us before. He dodged
around our feet catching moths that had come inboard on a
south-east wind. The wind fell, and we found light and heat on
the uplifting forecastle head, where Tommy tried to photo-
graph dolphins coiling in the transparency before the ship's
nose. He was, this fine day, in hearty agreement with me on
one thing; for the Mediterranean is now fully up to the mark
of its romantic holiday posters. This forecastle deck, the eyes
of the ship, is cluttered up with rusty and greasy gear. It is
bone-dry, with white encrustations of salt. The rust today is
vermilion. The seams of the deck timbers ooze blobs of tar

under a direct sun. There is that smell of dried dulse you notice on a summer beach at low tide; and the buoyancy of the deck makes us feel of no weight as it lifts over turquoise swells that would be unseen, except that they have purple hollows. We are isolated and enthroned on air.

"What's the matter with earth as God made it?" Tommy asked.

The dolphins had been too artful for him. He was looking to Africa, and that was only tinctured gossamer to starboard. "There's a turtle," he cried. "There, you can just see his nose."

I saw it. The turtle sensed the push of the ship's stem and dived. It removed its spot of imperfection from the lustre of the sea. Nor was there anything in sight to remind us that other men were not as we were, entirely occupied in praising the bounty of God. True, one hour before there had been an aeroplane, which was not recognized, and it accompanied us a little too long; and at the same time a ship of war appeared on the horizon, and caused an anxious officer of the watch to send for the captain. One never knows, these days. But these blemishes had vanished, like the turtle. So I agreed that there is not much to complain about in the general show of our planet. Certainly it has unpleasant surprises, but most of them are put there by our fellows in the name of progress. Our vast alterations in the look of the earth, I reminded him, first showed on the shores of this sea. About here were devised the copper and iron tools and weapons, with which, in due course, the State was built up and elaborated, with its taxes, wars, and compulsions we do not always find as lovely as peace, roses, and pomegranates.

"And art too," Tommy added. "Don't forget that. Don't forget Greece. We're going there. I suppose you know Athens?"

"No, I've always dodged it when I've been this way."

"What? Cut out the Parthenon? Don't say that."

"Yes. I would not look. I did not want to be disappointed."

"Well, you're a fine fellow! And always reminding me of some tradition or other!"

"You and I had better confess. You know, as I know, that in our day keeping faith with oneself is not much easier than keeping a candle alight in a gale. And I've been watching events longer than you. That is why I dodged Athens. I didn't want to lose that dream. But I shall ascend the Acropolis this voyage, as you are in support."

October 20. Though there is Monte Carlo, Rapallo, Capri, Ragusa, Taormina, Malaga, Jaffa, and Alexandria, names abound in the Middle Sea which mean nothing to most of us. How little we hear of most of its islands! Yes, of the great majority of them. We passed yesterday the island of Sembra, off the Gulf of Tunis, a high mass of rufous rock, in which the setting sun gave away a central geological fault, with the strata vertical on one side of the fissure and horizontal on the other. The island was steep to the waters. It seemed without life, a fragment detached from the moon; and then we had a glimpse of a minaret rising out of a group of white houses. Who lives on Sembra? There is not a word about it in the books. Pantellaria followed, though after dark, and I suppose we saw it in its quiddity, including its political prisoners, for it was only a black smear under the stars. The stars were more precise. They trailed reflections on the sea. We were heading for the dagger of Orion hanging low in the east, and the Pleiades swayed about our fore truck. And this morning Gozo is abeam, and close in. It does not seem habitable. The talus below its cliffs, and its bald and arid plateau, boulder-scattered, give it the appearance of a rubbish-shoot; but there are signs on it of a prehistoric occupation which remains a mystery. Comino followed, and then Malta. The buildings of Sliema and Valetta, ascending in regular strata from the sea as pale terraces, suggest that they have been sculptured out of the island's limestone by the Cyclops.

I have loitered in Malta before, but did not care much for it because I had no money. Today also is disadvantageous, for this is the Sabbath, and one might as well hunt for refreshment in a Scottish village on that day. And you want refreshment, after the clogging diet which is suitable, it is supposed, for sailors. All we could get ashore was tea, and that mostly was tepid goat's milk; enough to turn one against any island. Nor was there any fruit, to remove the taste of a ship's grease. Damn Malta's innumerable goats! I suspect it is their fault the island is largely herbless. Goats will eat match-boxes and old boots while waiting about, and in sufficient herds they will change the prospects of a verdant land into a perishing desert. They can alter a climate by clearing a country of its green leaves. Then the gentle rain, in seasonable quantity, evolves into unexpected violent cloud-bursts that wash away the soil and leave in course of time the naked rock staring at a brazen sky. It is not for nothing that the stare of a goat has the fell expression of the father of lies. What is left of the trees and shrubs of Malta appear to be regretting existence, but they do their best, if they can find a crack in a vertical rock.

The island is unlucky in another way. It is visited by so many ships that its traffic obscures it. What everybody takes for granted is overlooked. Attention is drawn to the attractiveness of a familiar object only when it is not in its place. It was not until Mr. Herbert Morrison drove the first glad pick into old Waterloo Bridge that it became, too late, worth considering; until then it was merely a north and south roadway. One would have to stay long in Malta to learn the worth of what is there. The various *auberges* of the Knights would leave an artist and architect no time to ponder the scattered signs of people who lived here before Memphis was built. A boy tending goats near the ramparts of Valetta had the profile you may see in frescoes at Knossos. What was his line of descent?

At sea again, near midnight, a sirocco was blowing. I don't know whether our ship's movements could be called rolling and pitching, but a chair in our cabin turned a double somersault. It would have turned more but it crashed against the door.

October 21. She continued to roll all today, and her antics grew worse till near sunset, when there was some ease. If St. Paul's euroclydon was the same as the wind that upset us, then I am not surprised his ship had to be frapped. I quoted some facts about this from the 27th chapter of the Acts to our captain, but he was not impressed. He merely remarked that, so far, he had had head-winds out of every port. And, he asked politely, would I take the Orient Express home from Istanbul, and let him off? All sailors believe in the story of Jonah, and would cast lots today when in trouble, but for the electric telegraph.

The waves are short, steep, and tumbled. The air is hot and damp. Even Tommy is despondent, and muttered once that, for his part, anybody could have life's rough stuff who wanted it. He didn't. The moisture weeps from the beams of our cabin, in which everything is adrift. Moreover, the flies have come to us for shelter and company, and they are sluggish crawlers in this weather. Late this afternoon we passed the Italian steamer *Irania* loaded high with aeroplane bodies for Africa, which is poorly off in community-shatterers. She came out of the thickness at us as if determined to make us reduce speed while she crossed our bows, but our bridge wouldn't have that; we had the right of way, and held on. It was the Italian who flinched in the conflict of wills, and altered course to go astern of us.

I was reading a passage in Thucydides which had put me in mind of politicians and populace at home many centuries later —a cheerful echo in which to put down one's classic at night— when in came Tommy. He had been listening to the news. He then said, "Arthur Henderson has passed out." Uncle Arthur was a wise and honest man, firm in his Christian faith. The betrayal and treachery of that 1931 election would have broken the heart of a saint.

October 22. The Mediterranean is as fickle as some of the people who add romance to its shores, but there are days when its radiant innocence would persuade you that evil is no more. This is one. Was there a sirocco yesterday? When we had Cephalonia in sight the Ionian Sea was on that plane to which poets rise when they are in the heights and the right words find them. The young day was still and fair, the waters illusory, the coasts lofty, spectral, and legendary. It must have been Hellas we saw. Only our steamer and its routine belonged to the clock. While we were still grateful for this perfect approach, and thought we could make out Ithaca, the steward came to the bulwarks. He reminded us that over there was the home of Ulysses. From his further remarks, while he leaned on the rail, we learned that he knew things pertaining to Greece that were unknown to Homer. He freely reported much that scholars would have been astonished to hear, though they might have asked for more of his stories. He then left us.

"I wish," muttered Tommy, "that he had not spoken."

"He told the truth, as well as he knows it. There's your realist for you."

We put into Patras. For the first time, we ourselves were to land on Peloponnesus. The mountains on the opposite shore of the gulf come down sharply to the sea, and leave but a narrow foothold for the villages below. Lepanto is over there, and Missolonghi. Alongside the *Zircon* is another steamer loading Christmas fruit for London out of a fleet of Greek caïques. They have lateen sails, and lines almost as ancient as the *Odyssey*, lines only adopted late in the story of British sailing craft as a brave development in our naval architecture, round about 1850. It must be reported, however, that the smallest caïque now has a motor-engine to get her along when her wings are folded. Beyond again, yet too close, was a French steamer. She was discharging bales of dried cod from the Newfoundland Banks, and her stench was at variance with the morning light, though almost as widely diffused. We escaped from it into the town, though I should like to have stayed to learn the measurements of the best of the caïques; those little things look crank, but they suggest daring speed, and their men must be sailors.

We enjoyed ancient Patras, though I don't know why. Perhaps because we supposed it was resting content with its past, for its roads were rough tracks, and as casual as the wandering chickens and children. Men were hammering articles out of copper as if the busy age of that metal were now, and not at the back of Troy. On the mountain above the shore, by the ruin of a monastery, the air was strong with terebinth as we surveyed Achaia south of us, a wild of abrupt and tumbled heights, with Erymanthus superior, where Hercules destroyed the boar. Turning about, the mountains of Aetolia and Lochris were beyond the ships and the gulf below. I thought I saw why my friend Nevinson loved this country, and it was worth the climb to learn that. Perhaps if now I were only beginning I should have to choose between this land and Spain; or else China. Life isn't long enough to enter into all of it. As I am placed, I must look on, imprisoned in ignorance, like those political prisoners we saw on the way down to the quay again, conversing through iron gratings in stone walls to their friends outside, while soldiers with fixed bayonets stood by. Thucydides would have read that scene in a glance. He knew all about it. Within an hour of landing we discovered that in this country also a dictator, probably on behalf of its king, has been attacking the use of reason as if it were only an unsuitable poison for dogs. It begins to look as if men everywhere, for a few years, are to be lost in a state of hysteric trance, induced by dread of the very privilege which puts them above their sheep.

Lower down the slope from the prison was a junk shop, and in it we found an early edition of the *Voyages of Captain Cook*. How did that get there? What had been its adventures? A much more interesting speculation, that, than theorizing over the capers of humourless and implacable dictators. And I was the more sure that common sense would come into its own again, some day, when we seated ourselves in a pleasant room near the quay, hoping to get civilized food, but prepared for anything. We wanted, if we could, to miss the tinned sausages and what-not of our ship's table for one day. In that Greek dining-room we felt at first out of the picture; but the host was kindly. He came over and assured us gently that all would be well. He had English and French. He recommended dishes, and pointed to a wine he thought would be right. It was quite right, and after a trial we begged another bottle, and asked why it was unknown in England. He told us that it was Rigoty, a Patras wine, excellent stuff, but it hated travel. That is the

tender nature of many good wines. You must go to the vine-
yards for them, and drink the juice where the sun raised it.
Rigoty is tenpence a bottle. Patras has more than one good
point.

The opposite coast stood up nobly to see the last of day as
we put out from Patras; and then we settled down to read, but
our cabin had several visitors this evening. A few of our happy
company had discovered another local tipple, and they brought
it along to share it. This wine was red, and it sparkled. So did
their conversation. Tommy and I learned more of the inci-
dentals of war and revolution in an evening than we were
aware ever disfigured the importance of history. It is a pity
that what seamen chance to witness of these affairs loses itself
in the air of cabins. For that reason, we had never heard till
the wine flowed of Smyrna as it was in 1923, when the Greeks,
soldiers and women and all, were crowding down into it from
the hills, the Turks after them, while the city was blazing.
British seamen were looking on from the bulwarks, and did
what they could to help. It could not be much, but they saved
many. On the whole, perhaps it is better not to know much
about it. Our statesmen in London encouraged the Greeks to
that madness, which ended in horror that is safely hidden from
common knowledge. Another man with us had been in the
Black Sea during the Russian revolution. There seems to be
much in a revolution that attracts no attention. He spoke
regretfully, and at the end of a long relation, of one astonishing
occasion, never to be repeated. "Ah," he sighed, as he left us,
"they were hungry. You could buy a Russian princess for a
ship's biscuit."

When our visitors had gone we went out into the night,
where the air was fresher; as fresh as it was in the beginning.
Our ship was trivial beneath high coasts close to either beam,

the shadows of mountains over the Gulf of Corinth. There were lights strung along the shores. We had been looking at the chart for navigation in these waters, and it was alive with such names as Delphi, Helicon, Eleusis, Salamis. What is there to say about that? It is better, and easier, to say nothing. It was enough to see that the shadows of those superb shores easily support their legends and fame. If the evil that men do lives after them, to be paid for by the innocent, so does the good, to be enlarged in the year when remorse begins to work again. Better remorse than nothing.

October 23. Near sunrise we rounded the isle of Salamis for Piraeus. To the south of us the isle of Aegina was a bluish sea monster notched along its back, but larger than I expected to see it; and its distance told me in a glance that I had come to Greek waters too late, and should get no more than Moses did from Pisgah. Well, Moses was lucky to finish with that, and I am lucky to get this with Tommy beside me. Dared I have asked for so much?

Our ship made fast, and we landed on the threshold of Athens—concrete, of course—amid stacks of gas-pipes, cased motor-car bodies, sheets of galvanized iron, and drums of paint and oil. Though we did not land as easily as that. We had to wait aboard till the police had arrived, and had examined our passports, upside down. The police do that everywhere we go, and they are armed. You must wait. Forty years ago in this sea my passport was asked for nowhere but at Tripoli of Barbary, then under the rule of Abdul the Damned; and his examination was perfunctory. The police and customs officers, all that time ago, cared nothing for what I was, or what I had with me, but put doubts aside with eloquent hands, and were friendly with advice. They had no fear of strangers. We had

freedom then, but did not know it. Today, without the cre-
dentials of papers, signed and sealed, you dare not move; you
are worse than a criminal; you have no right to exist. This
exactitude over our identities is as if Authority has grown as
suspicious as an aged and timid spinster, who sees a burglar
whenever a bowler hat passes her window. Heaven knows
what would happen if we set foot on foreign concrete—which is
just the same as our own—and began to walk about stacks of
imported gas-pipes, unless an armed officer had sternly examined our papers the wrong way up for signs of Bolshevism;
and had stamped them because he did not know what else to
do with them. Men with automatics on their hips guard our
gangway wherever it is lowered. All this is new to me, as a
traveller. It is possible that what this brave new world chiefly
needs is not more food, nor even fewer guns, but a lift to merriment. When are we going to awaken in happy laughter over
ourselves?

Our ship, always uncertain in port of the time she would
take to discharge and load, and subject also to the whimsicali-
ties of her headquarters in England, sent by wireless every
hour or two, is therefore jealous of the movements of her
two passengers. Reluctantly, she advised us to go away; we
could be absent, she grumbled, almost as long as we liked. We
did not wait, but were off, as the hardware rattled overside.
Piraeus with its cabarets and boarding-houses for seamen, and
the street stalls of its money-changers, overlooking a tangle
of tram-lines and mooring-ropes to the quays of the old port
with its fishing-fleet and shipping, did not detain us. That
musky and vivacious scene in a candid light is always welcome,
but you can see something like it at home. We boarded an
electric train for Athens. From its window I watched an aridity
of stucco houses, dust heaps, shabby palms, and tethered goats

fly swiftly past. I knew, unhappily, that it would be so, and began to spell out a Greek advertisement in the coach. Tommy continued to look earnestly at the dusty plain with its villas and goats. Presently he startled me with an exclamation of wonder. I turned quickly, but our electric speed allowed but a bare peep; factory stacks at once intervened. Yet I did see it, I saw it, so exalted that it was only just below the blue roof of day; the Acropolis. It vanished in an instant.

That phantom in the heavens above the factory chimneys was unbelievable. Might it not be better now to take the next train back to the ship? If we continued we might be overdoing it. We had seen it, even if it were not there. Experience tells us it is a mistake to follow a vision too far; that way madness lies. Perhaps what we had seen was only the projection of fond hope; a mirage. Or reverie had called up a spectre from the past. That was all. Celestial signs have been abolished.

My companion would not have it so. He is young and agile, and trusts his eyes. He had me out at the next stopping-place. After that, and within a few minutes, he himself began to suppose we really had deceived ourselves. There about us was the real Athens, the city of today, without a Parthenon. We found instead of it a market-place, which said outright, as popular markets will, that the life of the city was at a low ebb and was rated cheaply. The sidewalks of the street had many gaps; most of the paving-stones were missing. The butchers' shops were cheerless with flies and festoons of tripe. The furniture dealers with their ornaments for houses would have shocked the taste of a careless lodginghouse keeper. Pericles is dead.

We wandered uncertain of our whereabouts in a suburb where the walls of the villas were stencilled freely, not with the sign of Athena's owl, but with the Hammer and Sickle;

and I could not believe those markings came there with the permission of the tenants. On one wall this symbol of revolution was painted over the royal arms, so probably the King of Greece cannot keep his mind on ancient standards all day long. The hour had come to take a taxi out of this. We had better get it over. "I was always afraid of this," I was saying to Tommy, as the cab pulled up at the base of some tumbled stones, before the gate to a neatly railed path. A cab, in fact, landed us before the Propylaea, just as rain began to fall. The hills around the city had darkened, though they were not so dark as the clouds that rested on them. But never mind. At least we could see the Acropolis was abandoned; the rain had given the famous hill to us alone. It was a warm and gentle rain, and could have been only the silence in its descent.

I suppose there is no way to communicate those chance intimations which affect us most. We know they are important, but only for us, and as we do not know exactly why, their validity might be lost in speech. An adventure which leaves us staring at ourselves is above expression, except by luck. Even musicians fail there. One may know little or nothing of the glory that was Greece, but to look up at the Parthenon, even through rain, is to see an expression of spirit beyond the interpretation of scholarship, as great music is. That temple is for all of us. It is magnanimous, and includes the meek at heart with the wise and great, as majesty would, while surveying from its high throne the confusion of palaces and factories of a modern and amorphous city. But it was men who built it. Men have this quality in them. Against the overcast sky those immense colonnades still glowed, as if ancient fire were inextinguishable in the heart of their marble. The pillars were of no weight, but were dilated with their original fervour. The temple pavements were bright, brighter than the sky, as if

the god to whom the abandoned court was once dedicate
had left there the virtue of a more innocent day.

The rain ceased towards sunset; and the sun, for a few
minutes, peered clear through a break in the clouds, over the
rounds of the dark hills. That western light and the temple
looked across at each other from above the gloom of the
world. A pair of tortoise-shell butterflies sported with each
other through the colonnades. Two ravens stood at the base of
a column, strangely black and lustrous against its pillar.

But I was alone. What had become of Tommy? There was
something I wanted to say to him, but what was it? I then
saw him strolling towards me from the Temple of the Carya-
tids, apparently very happy. He stood with me, facing the
west. He saw the ravens, but was silent. As we went down the
steps, leaving it, we turned in homage for the last time, and
a falcon floated away from the frieze, aerial as the lines of
its eyrie. I had to touch my companion to bring him round.

We had to go. It was time to return to the dock. We found
it was hours since we took to this hill-top, and began to hurry
towards Piraeus, towards transport, tumult, and life. It was
night when we reached the dock. We made our way round
barricades of merchandise and tangles of steel hawsers down
a mile of straight concrete from which the workmen had de-
parted. Only cold arc-lights were there. One revealing light
stood over the berth where our ship had been that morning.
The berth was empty. It could not be true, though we could see
it was. We recognized items of the *Zircon's* cargo lying about.
The vacant water was black and forlorn. We were marooned.

When a seafarer ashore on a foreign coast goes back, his
head light with pleasant thoughts, to the quay where he left
his ship that day—and, whatever he may think of her, she is
his house and his support—and finds she has gone, his jaw

drops. For about a minute, that is all that happens. His jaw takes time to return to firmness and utterance. After some attempts at adequate speech, which are hasty and imperfect, at length he forms sizeable words. It could not be questioned. The *Zircon* had gone. We were on the beach, and at night, knew nobody there, and could not speak Greek, and the ship had our clothes, property, passports, papers, and money; it had everything down to our tooth-brushes. All of it was in a cabin somewhere in the outer dark, bound for Turkey. Also, the rain had been wet. We accosted a near ship with an anxious question, but she was Dutch, and nothing else. We found an aged Greek crouched within a recess of the cargo our ship had discharged, but he was as mad as we were.

Back at the dock gates again we ran into another Greek, a sailor this time, who thought he understood our trouble. He was confident. He took us in hand, and led us to an underground apartment with subdued coloured lights, a saxophone, a violin, and many languorous and softly spoken girls; and he seemed inclined to oppose our strong disbelief that this was the office of our ship's agent. The names of Greek streets are very unlike English, especially after dark, and it was only by good luck we found that office, which was closed, though it had an ancient watchman with a corrugated face of brown leather whose impassivity would have defeated the best of the Argonauts.

We gave it up. We did not feel equal to arguments with the police, and found a room above the harbour, where we hunted cockroaches a little now and then, and waited for morning. The lights of the harbour were some compensation. We could admire the scatter of many coloured stars, wonder what they stood for, and then turn to calculate, from a map, and the *Zircon's* knots, our chance of coinciding with her and our clothes somewhere between Salonika and Egypt. Towards day-break we arrived at the conclusion that this chance was about as far as the first prize in a large sweepstake, and that may have been the reason why we could not sleep; that, or minor matters, for the beds were dubious, but as good as we could pay for.

October 24. To be destitute is to be underfoot, but we were lower still; we had no claim to be alive. Without our papers we had no name, and no home, to say nothing of a nationality. Now we knew the taste of it. Before 1914 this accident would have been a joke, to be passed on. It is no joke this year. Un-less you can prove who you are without evidence, to officials who dare not believe you, but have to assume you are a bad lot or you would not be there, then you can neither stay in a place nor leave it. Where there is no freedom of movement there is tyranny; civilization now is wrongly named. After a long search we found the Greek agent of our ship, and he and his staff could only decide, after carefully accounting it, that we were in a fix. But the good man did introduce us to a resident Englishman, once an officer of the Royal Navy, a seaman to whom rescue work had been a commonplace of routine, and nothing for fuss. The habit of it had not left him. He took us to his place at Phalerum Bay, sat us under trellised grape-vines to moderate the sun, and fed us on red mullet, bread, dandelion leaves in olive oil, and resin wine, while we looked across blue water to Mount Hymettus. We did not care, while he yarned to us, whether we ever found the *Zircon* again.

Yet presently the dark thought did intrude once more that we had no name and no country; that we could not prove we had ever been born. Our friend was easy over that. Of course, he knew more ships than any shipping agent, because his interest in ships is large and intrinsic, and not commercial. Then again, having served under the White Ensign, he is not only a humanist, but a bold one, and shapes his battle tactics with a knowledge of facts withheld from the unobservant. He knew of a Polish ship. He thought she ought to be there that night, and sailing at once for Istanbul. He then sorted some bread crumbs with a knife, as if for divination, and deduced that, with her speed, she should find the *Zircon* in port. Till then we were unaware the Poles possessed steamers; anyhow, that they had one fast enough to overtake our ship, which had a start of two days. It seemed a long shot to us, too much for the science of the best of naval gunners. And the Greeks, we had discovered, could be doubting enough; but what would the Turks say, if we arrived in Istanbul with no evidence of positive existence beyond our vaccination marks? Turks are stubborn, and just then had no reason to rejoice over the English, unless found in misfortune. Leave that to me, said the navy man. This we did, and the Turkish consul at Piraeus, somehow, was less curious over our past than our own Foreign Office has been of late years. The Royal Navy has an influence which is mystical. We were made free to board the twin-screw *Kosciusko*.

Her size and quality surprised us. She was informative. It became a possibility that the Polish flag, so lately salted, could indeed overtake the Red Ensign, on our behalf. The notices she exhibited for the direction of passengers were in Hebrew and five other languages. Her officers had not the slightest doubt she could catch any ship afloat; indeed, we had not been aboard her one hour before we found that our knowledge of European economics and politics and of modern geography were but rags and tatters surviving from a forgotten year. The

Polish flag over us was proud in a new era that was rum to us; but the ship's usual brass birth certificate, giving her origin and year, always to be found abaft the superstructure, had a simple word of home, for it told us this liner was born in 1914 in the yard of Barclay Curle; and everyone who knows the sea knows that name. No wonder her Polish crew were proud of her! We met aboard a young Pole—yes, of course he was a Count—who spoke seven languages, and his business was to teach English to the crew. The liner's captain, an elderly, handsome, and courteous giant, approached us, concerned for our comfort in his ship. He had much to tell us of Polish mariners. As he continued his leisured and learned discourse in perfect English of the lore and literature of the sea I began to feel sure I had a card to win over this Polish ship-master; so when at last he did mention Joseph Conrad I said casually, playing my card on the instant, that I had known Conrad. But it was no trump. The captain of the *Kosciusko* covered it with the remark, "I speak fourteen languages."

October 26. We are in the Aegean, and till this day it has been no more than an attractive page in an atlas. We ought to have shipped for it in a caïque, I know, but we have done the best we could. We passed close to Homer's "lofty Skyros," where Rupert Brooke lies. In its way, our voyage was stranger than if we were early navigators, and lifting these islands for the first time; for the man is not born who would dare attempt a modern Odyssey. It would be only a senseless muddle, never transcending to wonder, and irony would be its note. As this year is so very late after Plato and Paul, perhaps the wonder of it is in just that very fact of muddle. Under the shadow of Lesbos, Syrian girls in sailors' slacks promenade the deck of this Polish ship. The island was not there for them, though Sappho herself come to life might be mistaken for one of the handsome nymphs, if in slacks. It was stranger still, while leaning on the rail of a Polish liner beside a Rabbi, to sight Lemnos, and Imbros beyond, and Cape Hellas, and to remember the fateful landing of a British army. The world is becoming bewilderingly mixed, though nationalism can be as rabid as an infected dog. Turks, Jews, Syrians, Greeks, and the rest of us, dress after the same fashions. We are very much alike, except in our hatreds. Only the Rabbi is a little different in his black gaberdine and black skullcap. A brisk and youthful Turkish officer with us, with his Hitler moustache and fair complexion, could pass at Aldershot for a nice British subaltern. The Turkish women about the deck would be unnoticed in Oxford Street.

And there to starboard is the Plain of Troy; near that point Scamander enters the sea. To port is Atchi Baba, and all along the shore are the white tombs of the Dardanelles Expedition, testifying to the heroism of common men lost in a later and greater war. The sunset was glory itself, but I fancied it had less to do with us, was more aloof than usual, as if our share of it were accidental. That may have been so, because its glow touched into prominence the graves ranged along the Gallipoli Peninsula, for the sun could not have been attempting a deliberate rebuke, as his revelation was meaningless to our light-hearted company. The meaning of those staring white marks had sunk to the same significance as the marks on the opposite shore of Troas, where men died for lovely Helen. Anyhow, the sun had witnessed it all, from the Wooden Horse to the steamer *Clyde* landing its British heroes; and we had better suppose, to be on the safe side, that there is universal remembrance. The Rabbi beside me, who remained as still as the shore he continued to contemplate, perhaps was regretting servitude in Babylon; or his evening thoughts may have been where moth and rust and sword cannot corrupt; he was a venerable man.

We were boarded in the Narrows by severe, sceptical and energetic Turks, armed, as ever, with automatic guns. We were crowded into the smoking-room, and subjected to so exacting a scrutiny that one could have been positive not a goat was left among the sheep; only we know how easily goats pass through, while lambs are left to bleat in vain appeal at the implacable gate.

October 27. I woke, with the fancy that the liner was much too quiet, and went on deck. Then there was no surprise that she was silent. She was at anchor. The coming day was announced to a sleeping city from the minarets of Istanbul. The dome of St. Sophia was glowing over our ship. But that was not what I was looking for, not so soon. I began to search, in a morning still very dim over the water, for a familiar funnel among those plentiful funnels and masts that had not yet come to life. I could not find it. I walked aft, in renunciation; and there veritably she was, at the buoys under our counter, the little *Zircon,* also asleep. The sight of her so near gave me liberty to be at ease while another day was finding all the spires and domes of Byzantium; the city could never have looked more beautiful than it did that morning.

October 29. Seamen have a view of the general scene as short, usually, as that of villagers who cannot help knowing more than they should of their neighbours, but who would not be unduly distressed if the cathedral in a neighbouring city, to which they seldom go, were burning. They are like most of us when we hear of flood and famine in China. The

men of this ship are incurious, except over the sounds that
issue from their radio boxes, and for those asides and merry
scandals that lighten the tasks of a ship's day. In fact, we are
human. When we tie-up anywhere our men seldom go ashore.
If they did, what could they do? They have no money. When
this ship touched at Constantsa in the Black Sea, we had to
display to visiting Roumanian officials our belongings, including a tally of our pocket-handkerchiefs; and, for some reason,
our spare cash especially interested those inquisitive officers of
state. The money of the forecastle, therefore, was exhibited
publicly in the saloon, and it amounted to £4, 10s. for 20
men. This can only mean they are not voluptuaries; should
they go ashore they cannot rejoice. All they learn of lands beyond alien quays is from hearsay, and myths grow funnier in
gossip.

They must have lost count of their calls at Piraeus, but are
content—they have to be—with their view of its docks over
the bulwarks; and its sheds and appliances are equal in love-
liness to those of Hull and Singapore. The captain himself
may journey briskly as far as his agent's office, which is round
the corner from the ship. The steward knows his way about
the markets, none better, and no Levantine will ever best him
at its stalls; and what he can tell you of attractions just back
of the quay, and of very many quays, is precise, personally
acquired, and would make Mr. Baedeker nervously adjust
his spectacles. Our able seamen and stokers know their element, and the ways of ships, and the ways of owners, with a
dry particularity which no Whitehall principal clerk could
acquire up to his pension year, despite his library of records
and statistics. Not one of our company, however, has been to
Athens, nor wants to go; not even Dicky asked what we saw
there. When south of Almeria, Spain, after sundown, I

pointed to a line of ghostly light in the sky far to the north, and said to our navigator, "That will be the Sierra Nevada." He peered at this landsman ironically. "No," he answered, "that's the Andes." Yet that man has seen the glow of the Andean peaks, for when an apprentice he was in sailing-ships which went for nitrates to the West Coast of South America, and he had plenty of time to speculate over the ethereal light in the sky of high snow and glacier, as he had rolled at anchor in the Pacific swell for months at a stretch. He and his like are concerned all day and night only with the signs relative to the safety of their ship in the present hour; with that, and engine troubles, and the monotony of the food.

Ah! that food scale prescribed by the Board of Trade! No doubt it is nourishing with scientific quantities of proteins and calories and what not; but it does not add to joy. For what about the cook? Our cook has to bake bread in a rush for thirty men each day; and that and the meals, aft and amidships, give him little time for sleep, to say nothing of art for the menus. "Fish-balls again?" cried Dicky jovially to the steward. "I'd sooner have them without so much cotton-wool for binding. Where's the black draught? Never serve fried fish-balls without black draught."

It does not surprise me that seamen are afflicted more than they should be with gastric ills. It is not strange that what they know of foreign places and peoples, though very interesting, and livelier, as a rule, than our reading in most books of travel, yet adds little to our certainty of the world beyond the Thames and the Mersey. I have noticed that when they return home they have nothing to say of a year in the foreign except an odd comment or two. This is greatly to their credit. They are more modest over their exploits, and their marvellous score of miles covered, than are we who write about our little occasional journeys.

Dicky knows I write. He has caught me at it. He is a reader, though chiefly of technical books, and he treats me with a touch of the deference in his affability which he would accord to a writer on naval architecture, and I do not deserve it. In his cabin today he was ironing his socks on a blanket laid on his desk. His canary, under whistled encouragement, lightened his task with song. The portraits of his family are about, but the most conspicuous ornament in his room is over his bunk, a picture of his first ship, under all canvas. He gazes at his treasure gravely, and recalls for his visitors a comic story or two about her. He is a poor hand at heroics. He was a lad when that ship was on the surface. Her captain kept hens in a coop for his own benefit, and had a lock and key to it, but the apprentices had the eggs. The bottom of the coop was vulnerable. Their master diagnosed that the motion of the ship upset the minds of his hens, so that they forgot about eggs, and the coop was slung in the rigging. The next night, when the boys were conjuring with it, the bottom of the coop fell out, and the birds flustered overside, with frenzied cries. The game was up. Dicky admitted that ships' apprentices in those days would have done anything short of murder for food; "though one or two murders wouldn't do a lot of harm on some ships. Yes," he reflected, "the men who ought to die don't. They are managing directors when we are drowned."

He did not altogether regret this. He guessed life was worth having while he had socks to iron, a watch to keep, and a pal to talk to. What did I think? Did I ever listen to the radio parsons? He had picked up one just now by accident, heard him for ten seconds, and then switched off the blighter. That superior voice, to a man doing a bit of ironing at sea, and wondering in what year he could get command of a ship, if ever, or better still, become a shore superintendent and live with his wife, tried Dicky's patience, it seems. I pointed out to him that the voice sounded superior probably because the unlucky speaker was nervous before the microphone. That was all. Moreover, some parsons never get a church, and many of those who do must sometimes wish they had a trifle of the benefits that go to managing directors. Dicky was getting a bottle out of a cupboard. "So you think it is bad for a man to be good, like me?" he asked, over his shoulder.

Tommy joined us. He had been down below again with the chief engineer, and knew more than he used to of marine engines, furnaces, and boilers. He showed proper respect for the men who design ships and build them. This touched our sailor. He can be gay about ships, and scoffs at sentiment; but, to him as to all seamen, a ship is a lady. Only her husband has the title to be rude to her. Because seamen will have it so, a ship is the only inanimate thing in English which is by custom honoured with the feminine gender. This can only mean that, beyond the economics and political necessity from which she arises, and the science which gives her form, a ship embodies the values which make pictures, music, and poetry; she is beautiful because she represents human aspiration adventurously. She is more than the cargo she carries, more than property, she is above the company of men who safeguard her. She is a person. This seamen admit, though not in words. They would never do that. But, at the call, they will spend their lives to save her. She commands a devotion given only to ideals that quicken the heart and make resolute the will.

It would have been hard to gather this from what our chief officer was saying to my son, but it was there. Dicky's voice was in a lower key; he was serious. He was explaining gross and register tonnage, dead weight, displacement, and freeboard. With the aid of diagrams and faith, we attended to abstractions, to metacentre, centre of gravity, and centre of

buoyancy, and other subtleties of a ship's body, never more
visible than the soul of a woman, but governing her behaviour,
and essential to understanding if you would serve her well, no
matter what the cargo, when she is stressed by seas and weather
at their worst. And all the time, she is to be coaxed along by
what our fathers have told us, and by taking counsel at night
of the stars.

The steward came in. He listened to the peroration with the
detachment of a sceptic late at a revivalist meeting. He then
asked whether it wasn't true that a navigator with an extra-
master's ticket, and forty years of service, responsible for the
safety of a million pounds' worth of property, to say nothing
of a thousand lives, might be rewarded, as a noble bloke, with
a trifle of money, never to be increased, which would send a
stockbroker into a nursing-home for repair to his self-respect.

The converse then lapsed. We became nonsensical. Only
the canary maintained its gentle soliloquy, as if morning were
always with us, bright and innocent.

DICKY. Well, what did Captain Cook get for discovering
    Australia? Not half the rake-off of a smoke-room
    steward on one Atlantic run. Don't forget what hap-
    pens to sweepstakes for the passengers.

STEWARD. Why shouldn't it? Quite right, too. Doesn't the
    steward give fun? That's better than convicts at Botany
    Bay. He ought to have a good rake-off.

DICKY. You've got a low mind. That's what comes of
    doctoring old tinned stuff to make it smell fresh. Talk
    about fun!

STEWARD. I wish I was a smoke-room steward, running
    sweepstakes. They're fresh each day. They pay better
    than tinned tripe for grousers who can't taste the dif-
    ference from fresh, anyway, but pretend to.

DICKY. All right. We'll overlook it this time. I expect we'd
    die of knots and bends in the guts a day or two sooner,
    if it wasn't for you.

The heads of these two men had the salient profiles of de-
pendability. If trouble came, you would be glad to see them
near. They would know what to do next. Though both of
them had survived occasions in the war which they took to
be a finish, they were droll and allusive about it.

Tommy asked them to explain a whisper he had heard below. One of the stokers had seen that man again, in an alley-
way, coming out of a bunker. What did it mean? Who is he?
They wouldn't tell him, down there.

"Ah!" said the steward. "That's the trimmer who never
signed on. They say they see him, now and then. I never do.
I don't feed him."

"He's only one of the things that help to keep us alive," said
Dicky. "We must have 'em. It's all the religion we've got. I'd
see ghosts if I had to shovel coal all the time in a bad light
while pouring with sweat, and no beer."

He was doubtful of apparitions, while not denying them.
He thought no seaman should deny them. A sailor ought to
know he never will know enough to go far with his denials.
He remembered then something of his topsail schooner, when
she was a Q ship. He was off Cherbourg hanging about for
submarines, not really hoping one of the beasts would find him,
but ready for it if that happened. He was boarded by French
officials. He was not dressed as a naval officer. He was in the
usual old togs, with a choker round his throat, and trusted
he looked the part of an ignorant scoundrel. While he commanded that ship he was nobody, and was going nowhere.
But the Frenchmen did not accept his rigmarole. They were

worried. He wouldn't have believed his story himself, from another man, but he couldn't give the show away. Still, he didn't want to be taken into Cherbourg, under arrest, wasting time. The dissatisfied Frenchmen went to the cargo hatch, and cast off the cover. They saw below in the gloom of the empty hold fifteen bearded ruffians sitting round the light of a hurricane lamp, playing cards, and fled overside instantly; they dropped into their boat and were away. They were scared. Dicky didn't know what ailed them till later. Whenever he was asked the name of his ship, he always had a new one ready. It was his practice to find a new name for her every night, usually out of his own head, but out of a book when tired. The name he gave to those Frenchmen chanced to be that of a schooner sunk off Cherbourg three weeks before.

October 30. We are at Ismir. It used to be Smyrna. The Turks prefer their own name for it; but we are told it was one of the Amazons—they used to live hereabouts—who named it Smyrna, so it must be very very old. We approached it in an early light. Its white-terraced homes face the gulf within an amphitheatre of mountains, and one has to admit that the old Ionians had an eye for the site of a city. As worshippers of Diana they showed their good taste. This is the last of their famous cities. But when we went ashore we were soon reminded that the Ionians have gone. Since the day when Diana ruled at Smyrna, men have been doing their damnedest for Belial instead, and not too badly. We have been picking up, throughout the voyage, a word here and there of the doings in this city after the Greek defeats in Asia Minor ten years ago. Multitudes of refugees poured through the mountain passes to this water-front, from which only ships could help them further. Our navy knows something of what

happened then, but has made no report. The city still betrays
what the background was to those quays, when a host thronged
the sea-front, waiting to be taken away. Much of it is rubble
and calcined walls. Fire has been through it. We found the
old British consulate, but it was no different from the rest of
the sad wreckage, except for its metallic plate with its proud
emblem the worse for the furnace. No doubt the city will rise
again. Life has a generous drive; we get another chance. This
may be so because a creative purpose unknown intends not
to let us off till we have done something more becoming; and
evidently it is patient, and eternity is long.

Smyrna's streets are as if one of its earthquakes had erupted
the footpaths and they had not been replaced, but we were
told this is but their proper condition. The hollows in the roads
were pools of water. Paving was for breaking the ankles. Yet
most of its people were in the last fashions of Western dress;
we saw only two women wearing black and the yashmak. In
the labyrinth of the bazaar, where men were busy at their
many crafts, and where round a fountain under a mosque a
confectioner displayed his cakes, one still hoped to find the
character of an older city; but the variety of the past is hardly
ever seen now, in Smyrna or elsewhere. You might as well look
for a smock in Sussex, or find a Newhaven fishwife as handsome in her own style, creel and all, as when an English king
praised her. From Shanghai to Istanbul, people are merging
into a uniformity as featureless as the woolly flocks; as if we,
too, were mass-produced, like our opinions, our habits, and
our flats. When humanity is ruled by some general notion more
or less, the world over, and lives on the same synthetic foods,
mostly out of tins, and depends on chemists instead of cows
for butter; when we have agreed about films, novels, radio,
politics, and God, and prefer to fly about instead of loafing and

inviting our souls, then all promise will have gone from life's experimental variety, and the hour come for the earth to be abandoned as past hope. And we shall have asked for it. There is no excuse for sameness and flatness. It is a crime against the intelligence. Uniformity is the abortion of creation. It is not harmony, but monotony, like the drone of our engines, and numbs thought. It means the death of freedom of the mind, and so the end of the soul's adventure; the hopeful old story of our beginning in a garden will be empty of its purport, for the spirit will be frustrate, good and evil the same, and our eyes blind to the glory of the Lord, should it be revealed.

The earth itself is never the same for one hour. That should be enough to warn us, if not to give us the humility to kneel. No scene of it is ever constant, but is as versatile as phantasy. We exist in a dissolving view. The outlook most familiar to us, the one we know best, the home street or hillside, will at times tell us, with a new light on it, that it is beyond our understanding and that its worth is in an unmeasured dimension. Smyrna, with the heights around it, and the gulf before it, changed, while we waited on our ship for departure, as if it were several cities in a brief space, as if it were still experimenting with the original unsettled intentions of the Ionians who were there first, uncertain which to be. The mountains about it, as variable as the clouds, ascended to the sky, or diminished, were of near thunder or remote gold, as the winds chose. And when our anchor was apeak, and we turned to westward at evening, it was daring of our ship to venture her weight into the rarity of the splendour beyond her iron prow. It was natural then to reflect with content that that night she would be threading the Cyclades and the Sporades, as if our course were among the stars; as if in the middle watch we should be dodging the points of the Milky Way.

November 1. A warm morning, with an inquisitive robin on a hatch, and a shy bird in the rigging; Tommy calls it roller. This is summer. All our ports are open. The wind is following, and our smoke leans over forward, lazily, as our speed is about that of the wind. There is a tapping of hammers; men are sprawled about the deck, chipping it. Egypt is in sight, and at noon Alexandria was just visible, a shimmer on a low and pallid coast. The ponderous mounds of water heaving past us shoreward are the glassy pale green of shallows and a sandy floor. The sea under the distant land is a long line of turquoise. "Egypt does not look as old as we've been told," said Tommy. He stood at the bulwarks, bare to the belt, a chipping hammer in his fist.

Dark antiquity? No, it was as bright as the hour, like himself. Age is only in the mind, and I wish I could always remember that. For if Egypt could announce itself as if it had only just arrived, then one's first instinctive morning elation is right, whatever the news of the day to follow. The pilot boat plunged about alongside violently, and the pilot was soused as he boarded us. When we neared the breakwater the surf was breaching it. Egypt was both vigorous and brilliant.

But what a warning of the day's news was sheltering within the breakwater! Battleships, cruisers, destroyers, an aircraft carrier, and transports flying many of the chief British house-flags, as though war were tomorrow, if not already upon us. Was it upon us? Had we missed the word? We learned, however, that Italy was only attacking Abyssinia at the moment, but that she had an army on the Libyan frontier three times the size of the British and Egyptian forces. Nobody was greatly concerned. Why, we are asked, is not Italy refused the use of the Canal? If we are really serious, why halt at a few tuppenny sanctions? We found less fear of Italy here than in London, though I should say I have heard only the opinions of British captains and officers; nothing from the Egyptians. Our navy appears to have a slight and casual regard for the Italian fleet, and whether that is through old pride or the latest knowledge I cannot say; perhaps it is of both. Native Cairo, of course, would have another mind about the matter. Cairo is wide open to bombing, for one thing, and anyhow its arguments would be Oriental, and hard for us to meet, to judge by the difficulties raised over our cameras, and by the arguments and searchings at the dock gates. It appears we are to understand that Egypt is for the Egyptians. Certainly, for who else has a right to it? The trouble is that Egypt standing alone could not save itself from being the Italian granary on an Italian sea which Mussolini has declared her to be, by nature and by his will. It tickled the *Zircon's* men to note that, while a fleet of ships in our dock basin slept in the dark at night, one Italian liner stood out brightly, a searchlight turned on her flag aloft. She might have been anxiously expecting her friends in another hour. On the other side of the quay British sentries guarded war stores. Whatever the news in London may be of the success of well-inspired diplomatic action, in the Mediterranean ruder notions are fingering the triggers. War appears to be round the corner.

Cairo. We have been in Cairo two days, but have not found it, so far, though the animation and smells in the market are promising. The market is always the place to make for in a new city; there the strange people are, without constraint, and signs of the way they live. Cairo's markets make us regret we know no Arabic, and did not live here. You don't regret that in the hotel, nor anywhere near it. Still, our hotel has an enclosed garden, and there, early this morning, before the sunlight had reached the ground, when only the crowns of the palms were in day—several date palms, and one royal—we were glad we were in Egypt. We had the garden to ourselves. We could see we had surprised the plot. We were not supposed to be there. A sentinel kite watched us. We may have been watched otherwise, but saw no eyes. Turtle doves made the silent brightness dreamy. The garden was in that pause in time when, free of the confusion of dualism, you realize with a start that you are present, you yourself, as if by chance the unseen barrier had been passed, and you are in the forbidden expansion where reality is no mystery. All is clear, down to the fact that hitherto unconsidered sand-beetles, busy at your feet, are gems. The ground you walk on is alive. The palms are tranquil in their knowledge. A hoopoe is there, crest erect, as confident as a familiar, moving about so fast yet delicately that we see it is careful not to interrupt the humour of the moment.

A dragoman has attached himself to us. At first we were firm. We did not want him. But he was firmer. He spoke English with a turn that I knew, so I had to ask him where he found it. He was, he said, in Palestine, in Allenby's Camel Corps, and stopped in the street to confirm this, uncovering a livid scar in his leg gravely and proudly. As he stood well over six feet, and was as heavy and active as a sergeant of the Guards, I judged I had been as firm with him as I need be. Moreover, Tommy thought we should like him. He had the candour and cunning of an old soldier, and might be of help to us, as he was a Mohammedan, when it suited him. We soon made use of his religion, for he took us through the mosques with so easy an access to their treasures that the Prophet might have franked us; and though I was as prudent as ever when in a sanctuary, our guide's bearing gave us the

broad idea that desecration is not what it used to be. Perhaps
he felt that a friendly understanding between men who had
shared the same war is religion enough; or that the trust of
friends supersedes acknowledgment of the ineffable, at a pinch.
We found afterwards that we remembered of those mosques
little except the graciousness of the glass lamps pendant from
the heights. This fact made Ali frown, for he had not supposed till then that the lamps were worth a thought. "Right
you are," he said. "I know where I can find one." He
could find anything we wanted, and some things we did not
want.

It astonished and saddened him that our interest in the
Pyramids could never be found. His pride was hurt. He could
not approve our preference for unconsidered trifles, for no
more than loafing by the Nile, watching the unloading of
grain from river craft. The lateen spars of these vessels raked
up to a hundred feet—the height and daintiness of those spars
at night were unbelievable, black threads meshing the stars—
and their fine modelling was most satisfying. The bronze tor-
sos of the men working on them, the broad water of the
famous river, and the sun, made us regret we could not charter
one of those ships, and dawdle along deep into Africa, as near
the Mountains of the Moon as her draught would take us.
That would be something like a voyage. Time would be left
astern and forgotten. But we could only look on, select the
craft most to our liking, and dream; though that was better
than an ascent of those antiquities in the sands beyond, the
eternal stones piled up as testimonies to pride and slavery, for
everyone to note; you cannot miss them; but we intended to.
One morning, however, Ali inveigled us far from the city on
some pretext or other, and unexpectedly, when we had no
thought of wrong, faced us with camels; supercilious beasts

that would test the capacity of the most generous lover of animals. He bade us mount. When Ali has us in a corner we find it easier, as a rule, to give in and take what comes than to argue.

We were fully content at the time in a village by the river. The weekly fair was being held, and the assembled fellaheen put us more deeply into history, well back towards the First Dynasty, than one ever is in a book or a museum. The village was a huddle of flat-roofed mud houses, and a mill. The smell of the flour was characteristic of the place, and usually it over-came the other smells, and they were many and some of them strong. The irrigation areas around the village had to be crossed on stepping-stones. Tall palms overshadowed it. The narrow passages between the dwellings swarmed with children, sheep, goats, and flies. Occasionally an alley was blocked by a camel taller than the walls. We saw a partial plague of flies, and understood why ophthalmia is usual. Donkeys were being paced, where there was room for it, and it was clear the judges were rigorous about the points of a donkey. Buffaloes as rounded and black as basaltic boulders, and as still, were half-submerged in ditches. Ancient Egypt was about us. We could hear it as well as smell it. Bold wenches lolled at portals, and beyond their doors the interiors were in midnight. Or the girls marched up from the river, black-gowned, balancing jars on their heads. The light of the Nile was behind them. Over the back of a buffalo a kingfisher flashed. Old women sat under decaying walls, and of so forbidding a countenance that it was a pity we had bought no amulets at the fair, where charms against the evil eye were being sold, and for other evils too, some so recondite that they boggled even Ali, or else embarrassed him. The men were tall and brisk, and I guessed could be an unruly lot if swept by an idea, but they were friendly with us, very likely because of Ali's superior height, and his composure and air of soldierly authority. I was not sorry he was with us. Nearly all the women were in black. There was a splendour of sun, but little colour, except the cerise and orange frocks and silver ornaments of the little children.

We were admiring a file of lordly geese step past, every feather as sharply defined as in a primitive fresco, parading in state as formally as a ceremonial poem, when we were turned by Ali and faced with two camels. I did not want a camel, but the monster allotted to me kneeled with a groan. Its attendant, whose face I trusted no more than the sneering lips of my camel, then spoke to me in the vernacular of New York, which had been his home, he assured me. I mounted the unfamiliar beast without another word. A combination of Ali and New York is beyond my power.

Afterwards, when toiling up the squared stones of the Great Pyramid, I remembered Mark Twain had said he was up and down it in ten minutes. I remembered in bitterness. I do not call him a liar, but suppose that as a practical joker he arranged a trap to fool us. I myself was glad of the broad prospects from the apex, for more than one reason. Those blocks of syenite are three feet square, sometimes more, and often have no satisfactory handhold, and they recess upwards to the hot sun interminably. And why go up? I envied a painted lady butterfly sunning itself near my nose, for it could treat those steep and treacherous steps with contempt. How Tommy was managing it with his camera and stand I did not ask, for I did not want to heave skywards more than my dislike of this folly. In the descent I went first, and half-way down, while paused to recover balance, heard a fall above me. In that instant a dark object shot over my head and described a remarkable arc in its descent out of sight. I turned in horror. Tommy stood high against the sky, as though also poised for flight, and cried out that a lens had gone. Well, it had gone, but he hadn't. It would be hopeless to search for it in the waves of sand below, even if it had reached them. When we jumped to earth from the last step we all but landed on it; it had shot out clear, was without a mark, and was waiting for us. Would anyone who slipped well up that mass shoot out clear? The angle suggested it was possible. Ali thought they would, after a bounce or two. He said it had happened, now and then, though it was better to say nothing about it. Up and down in ten minutes!

The semblance of the Pyramids, dominant in the waste, and the thought of what they stand for, is not easily told. I suppose it isn't possible to admire the geometrical monsters, but they cannot be dismissed. There they are. Perhaps Mark Twain thought some gay disparagement of the solemnity of the past would do no harm, and might relieve the present of its lurking doubt of what is bold and confident but only brand-new; a common impulse, not always so gaily expressed. A secret lack of assurance can be shown in many interesting ways. I have heard it expressed, with no gaiety, by young French writers when talking of Anatole France, and by others speaking of Thomas Hardy, and remember an angry rejection by a clever young painter of Leonardo da Vinci's Madonna of the Rocks. Those ridiculous Pharaohs! That simpleton King Arthur! Old Hardy, the vulgarian and pot-house writer! I myself suspect the Tom Sawyer in the great American, the everlasting boy, was really awed by Egypt, though that is what he would never admit before Pharaoh; and I am glad of it, with a certain reservation.

A salute to lost endeavour, to a relic of human effort overcome by years and the elements, may be a mark of self-respect. We are all of the family. Time will have us. I cannot read the pencilled scrawl of the last entry in Captain Scott's log without humility. Failure? Yes, but his failure raises a doubt. Could I have done so well? A touch of piety before a broken memorial, as before a masterpiece, does us no harm. And there came the Sphinx; for since we were at the Pyramids she could not be avoided. Her picture is familiar, and she is recognized at once, with her wasted neck sand-blown by the winds of ages. She is only a queer story, a curiosity from which interest has gone. But she surpasses all the legends and descriptions. The longer we looked at her the more we wondered. She really appears to hold a secret beyond our reach. The figure is nobly proportioned, and in the poise of the head is majesty. Tommy remarked, "I thought she was only another monster. Why, there is no sculpture comparable with this at home, except the Lohan in the British Museum." I could not help fancying that to be alone with her, between her paws, before sunrise, might rouse a fear that not only would unearthly music be heard, but that she would move. Myself, I should be inclined to get down before the sun peeped over the edge of the desert to start something.

I had that doubt more than once in Egypt, even in sunlight. If the earth remembers all we thought and did, though otherwise we are forgotten, then the Nile valley, so much of it sand, mirage, and shining emptiness, is a region to be walked warily by those sensitive to the past. People have lived here continuously for perhaps thirty thousand years. There were ships on the Nile, not unlike those by Cairo today, six thousand years ago. When the Israelites were here, Egypt's priesthood, arts, and civility, were as old to Moses as the Athens of Pericles is to us. Moses must have been a man of parts to have released his simple pastoralists, all slaves, from the clutch of Egypt's knowledge and power.

We came to the last evening of our stay, and from an upper balcony overlooked Old Cairo in its plain, spaciousness in a fading but clear light. The air had a crystalline brilliance un-soiled by dust and vapour. The only colours were the buff and saffron of the city below and of the Nile escarpment, and the blue of the sky. It suggested in colour and clarity a lunar age, and that all the years were spent. Human aspiration, labouring to improve its lot, disappeared from it with the grass. The run of the escarpment, where the eastern desert drops to the valley, was sharp in foreland and talus for miles, remote but magnified. There was no movement. The Shepherd Kings went some time ago. It was in repose for eternity. The yellow zigzags of the battlements immediately below were long out-crops of weathered rock; our planet's bare bones were exposed. The superior domes and minarets of the mosques reflected the level light of this day as did the sand of the plain around, from chance facets of the past. It was more like a shining ap-parition than a city. It was the august spectre, visible only in that hour, of once-upon-a-time.

We went down to make our way through it, not quite sure of our direction, nor whether we should like it. In the old byways, at evening, it was often uncertain whether we were wandering through yet another cemetery, or were among dwellings. All grey dust is grey. We were lost in twilight amid shapes that were nameless; they had come down to nothing. We stopped once, feeling sure these heaps about us were burial mounds, when a child's face appeared in the shadow of a cavity. The dust was alive. In that arid expanse, where habita-tions were sloughing with the graveyards into universal sterility, the delicacy of that child's face with its questioning eyes was as hard to accept as a resurrection. We had supposed that this place had joined yesterday's seven thousand years, but it opened, and looked up at us with the eyes of innocence. That child might have been nearer the secret of the Sphinx than we were.

Much nearer. Egypt is appallingly older than history. To look backward to human origins is as awful as peering into the probability of human futility. We know that men such as we are employed the first Impressionists, and excellent artists they were, when bison and reindeer were hunted where we see Paris. It was the last glacial age that ended the reason for their art. The emptiness of that remote past returns but the echoes of our questioning. Reckoning by the vestiges in the rocks, history is but a matter of the day before yesterday. And yet, though men were using flint tools for uncounted ages before they came to an alphabet, human existence is but a recent event in the story of the earth. Humanity has not been here more than a few weeks, as the stars measure time; and historically we are but just reaching the point where we surmise that we have yet to discover the things of first importance, if we would justify a continuance of our brief tenure. Tommy, sitting opposite in a hot and gritty railway carriage, looking out as we went back to Alexandria and the *Zircon*—supposing our ship were still there, though we should not have worried if she had marooned us again—suddenly exclaimed, as a modern impressionist would, "Look, Egypt is all a-growin' and a-blowin'. Who said she was a mummy?"

He was right, for anyone to see, and the Egyptologists wrong. They have not told us the first thing about the Delta. Beyond that train window, between Cairo and Alexandria, was a sensational prospect of vital abundance; not cerements, but fecundity. I have seen nothing like it except in Java. But that island is mountainous. In the delta of the Nile nothing is eminent save the rounds of white clouds, though the occasional mast of a vessel in an unseen channel points skywards. The land was uninterrupted in its march through clear distance to touch the lowest of the clouds. The clouds were as luminous as a multitude of great moons. They were stationary. They had nowhere else to go, but they had all that space in which to shine. We got an inkling of infinity. The sky was celestial and the earth fertile and serene.

We had seen all this before, in our outward journey, but it still astonished, a revelation of unending good. Where people were harvesting it was sere, but the prairie next to them was emerald with blades just coming through. There was no monotony in the peace and content of this land. An occasional minaret, instead of a ship's mast, indicated an unseen village. Sometimes we came to a canal shaded by tamarisk and mimosa. Egrets stood among the water-lilies. Camels with stupendous humps that were bales of cotton paced a road beside the water. Men were hoeing dried mud. Yoked oxen were ploughing. Maize stalks were being cut and stacked. Women in black strode along with pots and baskets on their heads. Buffaloes, all in polished slate and with bony behinds, went round and round drawing up irrigation water. Under a grove of mimosas a number of children were taking the shade with long-eared sheep, black goats, and white asses. Near a town—modern flats were going up amid the ruins of mud huts—was a compound, almost filled by a yellow hillock of grain. It stood at the back of a building with a name over it, The National Bank of Egypt. That was an object easily interpreted. There were no hieroglyphics about that. All banks are national in a sort of way, and well we know it. We felt no need to alight to ask what the result of so much sweat in the sun was doing in the back yard of a bank. Grain is golden.

November 11. The talk at breakfast in our mess was animated. There was an exchange of what each of us had witnessed at Alexandria of trouble in the offing. The seniors, having had a dose of war, showed no desire for more of it, but frowned and were silent; or said little, except to show aversion and perplexity, when the strange words and moods of Rome and a few other European centres were mixed with our ship's diet. Sparks once abruptly told us we need not worry about it, for soon all the world would either fight the Fascists or turn Fascist. Tommy heartily agreed with him. The master and Dicky looked at the table, and neither confirmed nor denied. I refrained from mentioning the last thing to take my attention at Alexandria; a British ship on the other side of the quay unloading ambulances. Right opposite me, on the saloon sideboard, the steward had placed a new and noticeable decoration, a vase filled with red artificial poppies. They had the sun. It was a morning of bright light. We are heading for the channel between Cape Bon and Malta. Some officers and men assembled aft. As the hour of eleven was struck on the bridge, the ship whistled, the engines stopped, and the ensign was lowered. There was no sound. This is Armistice Day.

November 20. The seas have gone down, to our relief, after a gale while crossing the Bay, but the swell from westward is awe-inspiring; we have small freeboard. As another range of water closes our beam, for our course is northerly, the serration of its ridge dancing high above our outlook shuts out the clear horizon darkly. At midday there is a bright sun, a clear cold air, and the Bishop Rock lighthouse in sight. There stands England.

It is no more than a slight exclamation mark. A little later we are abreast the Scillies, but those isles are frail and fugitive. When another glassy hill sweeps up and is past, going land-

II

The Practical Man

DECEMBER 1941. One of the Brains Trust, an eminent politician, asked the other evening what difference it would have made to mankind in general if Plato had never existed, answered boldly, "No difference at all."

He was prompt. There could be no doubt about this. Doubt may exist as to what flies do with themselves in winter, and anxious listeners still await a word on that; but listeners learn at once they need have no doubt about Plato's value to us. There isn't any. It would have made no difference had he been still-born. From this simple and honest answer we learn also that as our knowledge increases so we grow in confidence. A driver of a tank knows what Shakespeare never knew. In fact, not a senior boy at a technical school but might have answered the question almost as quickly as the selected Brain. That boy could have piped up with enough information to give him the requisite assurance, and full marks. He would have learned, in a lower form at school, and with pride, that not in all history has man shown such miraculous cleverness as today. The heir of all the ages, that boy would know what had never dawned in the best heads at the famous Academy.

The old Greeks, we are told, never challenged the gods, except by inadvertence, or in pride which had to be paid for; they allowed a riddle to existence, and feared to sport with it. We dare all, and have gained by it. We can see and hear that we have. Though Nature is as reluctant as ever, we have forced her to surrender. Anyone now can mount up with wings as eagles, without the aid of the spirit recommended by Isaiah; and on special occasions even higher, nearer the moon than ever, and then with artificial eyes destroy an invisible city below. So away goes the ancient awe of the unknown. We can say with truth that all Plato did was to deepen the mystery of existence. What good is that to us? How turn it to account?

Since philosophy, which is something near religion, can be dismissed at "the mike" with the indifference of a Nazi throwing petrol on books, we are free to ponder the secret winter whereabouts of blue-bottle flies, when not venturing appraisement—as today we must, for Rome must be taken—of the worth of the Sistine Chapel in terms of human life. As to the last, we are in rather a muddle. With philosophy dismissed, and a sense of right and wrong not quite at its best, it is not easy to measure an artist's masterpiece against one's love for a son, to discover the highest value. Probably the reason for this is that it cannot be done, anyhow.

If only we could have heard the gentle hesitant voice of Lowes Dickinson, an interrupting ghost at "the mike," immediately after the bold answer of the eminent live Brain! What comfort there! Then one could have switched off, happily superior, if a little dazed, to the worst that could come of all the present uproar in the world. But no such luck. We must do without ghosts and their voices, or most of us must. What really have we to go upon? Nothing much, except the faith that Plato's extension to mankind's outlook may be almost as good as the full benefit of the news this day on all wave-lengths. What difference to mankind has Confucius made, or Zoroaster—what difference any and all of the few superior minds? It is indisputable that Copernicus, Newton,

Lavoisier, Darwin, and so on, are not of much account at our street corners. For that matter, what difference has been made by the understanding of men and things of that best mind of them all—from Europe to the South Seas, where is the influence of Jesus Christ?

While considering this, doubtfully, let us admit that the speaker at the Brains Trust answered in accord with the spirit of his age. Athens is out. Bethlehem is out. He spoke as most would have spoken. It is right to acknowledge things as they are; but things are not always what they appear to be, that's the trouble. The implications of facts can be as occult as the subject the sirens made a song about; or let us consider, for a minute or two, what was inherent in the victory election of 1918.

Then again, what would have been said if the question, instead of testing Plato's contribution to general welfare, had sought the difference to us made by the explosive engine? How easily we can guess that! A parrot could imitate the solemnity of the reply, the hushed voice. Moreover, none of us can deny how much we should have missed if those lumbering gun-carriages had not quite suddenly grown powerful wings, taken to the air, and acquired the ubiquity of birds. The transmission to us of wisdom from the back of twenty centuries is not in the same class as the flight of a bomber. What is wisdom, and where is it to be found? It hasn't the ubiquity of birds and bombers, by the look of it.

One's relatives are in hourly peril. The Sistine Chapel is as likely to go as a slum. Nothing is exempt; not lovely innocence, not the promise of youth, not libraries of history and learning, not the glory of Chartres; nothing whatever is exempt that once justified human life; that itself is now as cheap as dirt. We are compelled to reckon many things anew. What has happened to us, as realists, since now we are driven to weigh the value of a masterpiece of art against our affection for mere persons? After we have come to the conclusion—rather surprisingly too, in the era of concrete and steel—that in art man rises somewhat above himself, and the noblest art is irreplaceable, if lost, we still feel that our friends are not of less worth. So what shall we do?

It begins to appear that, when deciding war to be far better than to allow our altars and everything else to be kicked over by perverts and morons, much that was inherent in the choice was not seen at the time. Good people, therefore, are now appalled, for they find that getting rid of German war factories also rids Germany of many women and children; yet evidently it has become a plain duty to destroy those factories. Every choice has its inevitable inherencies, just as though law governs our ways as well as the courses of the stars.

Since, as realists, we have to decide on abstract values and morals during battle, there is sure to be confusion and ambiguities. Those values have not been overhauled for a long time past. We have been too busy on other things, in the midst of progress, which had to be made. We never expected war to be so very bad that every treasure possessed by mankind would be threatened by fire and blast; yes, even the secrets of the heart, which may be the best of all. Young poets and artists are dying. Now it begins to dawn on us that things as they appear to be, at the moment when we decide as realists what to do with them, may have the very devil lurking in them, to be released by a false move. And how to know the right move?

Still, what else could we have done, after Hitler's act at Prague? What else was there to do but face him? Tell us that. It troubles us, the horror of it; but what is now going on in the world was as certain to come about as disease following careless dirt. Despite the uselessness of philosophy and religion, it is a pity that our statesmen, who in the past had to deal with things as they were, were not gifted with a trifle of that insight into reality which was native to Socrates. They are telling us now that nobody foresaw the consequences of war from the sky. But that is a lie. It was not only known but it has happened before. It happened in the last war. It was pointed out years ago that the cradle would have the place of honour in the next war; and it is there. Nothing is unusual about this week's problems of killing and destruction except this: that few people, even in Whitehall, hesitated thoughtfully over the hidden meaning of simple facts till London was burning. That the facts pointed to the destruction of Berlin was also unnoticed, if we may go by the speeches of Nazi leaders, who seem to be even more remote from Plato than our own.

III

Progress

JANUARY 1942. Some onlookers are sure the world of men, despite the newly acquired menace of its heaven, once its promise of bliss, gets better and better. I have tried to believe this, tried hard, but it is too much for me. My experience in watching the goings-on in that world has been fairly long, and my recollections as a journalist point to the probability that the commonweal, though its fund of skill, gadgets, and knowledge has increased miraculously in my day, makes collective noises more like Bedlam than ever, and louder.

An old friend in Fleet Street rebuked me severely one afternoon in 1938 for such an inauspicious view of human progress. "Look at the people about," he exclaimed, "how happy they are, and with all this hanging over them!" What was hanging over them was the shadow of Hitler's air-squadrons; and, as everybody knows, since then that shadow has not grown less.

I was inclined to retort on him with a story about my old chief, H. W. Massingham of the *Nation,* but refrained; for I am much attached to him, and suspected at the time that he was angry with me for confirming his own secret suspicion. Massingham, too, was hopeful of the best, yet was often sad over the evidence. In those far-off days there were peace conferences, Black and Tannery, the Geddes Axe, and so on. Something else blew in one day to dash my editor's hope. He pushed up his spectacles, and mournfully contemplated the office wall. "Man," he concluded, after this short pause for reflection, "is quite the bloodiest fool God made."

To show that my old editor had some justification for his remark, here now are some of our legislators, and a group of very important shipowners and industrialists, all sternly opposed to international control of the airplane. They insist on having what they call "freedom of the air." But do they know what they are talking about? Freedom for what? Because it is very clear that since man took to the clouds, and took up there with him rather less than the moral sense of the market stall, commercial freedom in the air may end in our inability to breathe it. There Europe is today, from London to Stalingrad, largely desolate, populations homeless and adrift, and faith in law as absent as in the Stone Age. Our latest gadgets have actually broken up the work of ten centuries. And the airplane is not fully fledged yet; its full plumage is to come. How will things be when it is absolute master, when it can get anywhere almost at once at short call, and no sanctuary from it remains on earth? Shall we become troglodytes once more? That would be a very rum consequence of our cunning, to be able to take fresh air only at night, and surreptitiously. Men of business terrify me more than Hitler ever did. As politicians, they are never right. Service of Mammon and the people at the same time cannot be done.

We should bear in mind that men of business have formed the bulk of our legislative body since the last war ended. Could a worse mess have been made of our affairs if we had left all to the luck of dice? Or even if we had closely studied to come a deuce of a cropper? Our relations with Europe were left to their hard and practical understanding of reality, and today we cannot even buy sweets for the children without official permission, to say nothing of entering Rome without risking the destruction of some of the greatest treasures of Christendom. Now these same gentlemen show annoyance because we don't feel like trusting them with the exploitation of heaven. But are they sure they could distinguish between Beelzebub and one of the hosts of light? They have yet to prove they know the difference.

All we do know about their discernment is that so many of them encouraged Mussolini and Hitler from the beginning, and would have no more to do with Moscow than the Nazis. Even Hitler's murder of Guernica taught them nothing. They did not rouse then to what was going on. Indeed, the signs of what was likely to come about were ugly enough in 1933. Then, however, it was only German Jews, democrats, liberals, priests, men of letters and trade unionists, who were being laid out; but perhaps there is not enough in that to indicate that English gentlemen could ever be treated the same way if a chance offered. Besides, those Bolshevists! So here we are. Innocence was due to be offered up, in the nature of things. But go on leaving our affairs to those same experts? I should not like the shade of Massingham to see that he was quite right about us, when with us in the body. Let his ghost pick up a trifle of confidence, on our account.

Yes, the oriflamme which Germany hoisted in 1933 was the head of Death. But that year was soon enough to decide what we had better do. There would have been no war, if good sense had been sufficiently general to have given Whitehall an expression to show it knew where it was, and what ought to be done; but we had only just elected to Save the Sovereign, and hadn't succeeded even in that. I suppose the trouble is that the citizen everywhere, even in the democracies, has lost control of his affairs; and if at the same time his Prime Minister insists on having sealed lips, then, though he may

guess pretty well that he is being led up Proserpina's garden
path, he must resign himself to Hades. Though we curse the
outcome of Totalitarianism, our own democratic legislature
has delegated much of its power. Office-holders do much of
the ruling of us, and with the usual tyranny of trifling intelligence not answerable to the courts of law.

The State and its edicts have been substituted for God and
a moral order. The State is an impersonal monster with a
heart of gun-metal and bowels of steel piping. Its only rule
is expediency. The citizen may vote, but the brute is still
there afterwards. The common man, nearly always and everywhere more honest and open to good sense than his leaders,
sees what has happened, and gives up. It was because he had
given it up that Fascism came in, to fill the gap, and profit by
his fears and resentments. The ordinary person may know per-
fectly well that the State is behaving in a manner which would
get him put away if he so conducted himself; but he submits
to cruelty and injustice, and even to doom, as if the worst
only were inherent in nature. He does not so much as grow
angry. He is aware that he might as well rebuke the weather.
With loose hands and will surrendered, he and his neighbours
submit to the damnable Engine.

If that is so with us, as it certainly was with the French,
what is the use of expecting the German people to rise against
their rulers? As persons, they are completely nullified. Perfect
Totalitarianism has seen to that. There is something else, however, about the Germans which is peculiar to them. They have
not only had personality and initiative drilled out of them in
the process of substituting uniformity for liberty. I cannot
myself make out what the characteristic is which makes them
peculiar; but Goebbels knows, and dares with it in a way
which would result here, I pray, in our own M.O.I. going up

in flames the morning after. I mean that queer happening after the catastrophe to German arms at Stalingrad. The German public was given the news; and then Goebbels turned on stately funeral marches. That looks very like a common gratification in self-torture. A more shocking warning of what a whole people may come to, when the State is Almighty, Omnipresent, and Omniscient, it would be impossible to find. Each one of us, to show his own spirit still is with him, had better go into the sanctuary of his choice, and alone, and light a candle, and remain in silent invocation, preferably on his knees, to show he is helpless, and desires grace.

IV

Back to First Things

MARCH 1942. The soldier was departing. His leave was up. We stood, the two of us, on a ridge above the Channel, waiting for the sun to show himself. The sky was kindling over France. We had not long to wait, only a few minutes more to be together, so there was nothing to say. Like others before me, the future unknown, I desired a token, some sign or another, anything would do, to tell me how things would be; but nothing showed in the sky but radial colours. I don't know what my companion was thinking. He seemed not glad to depart, but was silent. Very soon now, at the agreed signal from the sun, he would go on, to what he did not know, and I would turn back, to reassume patience while waiting for the same thing.

There came day. An arc of fire peered over the sea, and burnished it. Flames caught the clouds, and increased the zones of heaven. Athwart the bright plane of the Channel were arrayed the distinct black models of a convoy of British ships, stretching from Weymouth Bay beyond Portland Bill. "Asking for it," said the soldier, "but not getting it. What a target! We wouldn't have dared spread out so many in daylight this time last year. . . . I suppose we must be getting on. . . . But I wish America would tumble out soon, and pull her weight."

As to that I could promise nothing, except the certainty that somehow, somewhere, the pressure of opinion and desire would do it, to say nothing of the drive in enemy aims still secret, and America would be one indignant body in an hour. Then I stood watching that soldier's familiar figure as it descended the hill, and prayed, besides the advent of America, for other desirable but far removed occasions. No sign had appeared in the sky, nothing but the majesty of dawn; so the two of us that December morning were unaware, when the sun greeted us over the sea, that on his way to meet us he had looked down on the affair at Pearl Harbour.

The first word of it was as incredible as news always is of sudden madness where sanity was not suspect. But so also has been much else since the Nazis sacked Prague after making peace with it. We have to remind ourselves that those quaint Orientals, with their elaborate ritual for drinking tea and the adoration of cherry blossom, have done this before, and more than once. The Japanese had another advantage in the gracious stories which thankful travellers, who were men of letters, had created for them; and what a pity to waste it! The only certainty was that Japan had intended conquest, and America had not; and once more it had to be admitted sadly that when patience turns its back indifferently on plans for its undoing, the likelier the chance it will be upset. Then, within a little, we were caught, all unready, by the news that the *Repulse* and *Prince of Wales* had gone down in the China Sea. Such ships! And outside Singapore! The excellent method in Japan's madness was clear. The Nazis and the Japanese, helped by the disposition of Vichy's ships and bases, aimed to disperse our power by deploying in all seas. The fact faced us that the Japanese battle-fleet interposed between Panama and Australia. The enemy could choose where to concentrate, and we could not.

What would come next was easily guessed. Recrimination is now loud enough to be heard across the Atlantic. A babel of blame has arisen, and the greater part of the noise is from those who have never bothered to consider where the tide of events, from Versailles to Manchuria and on to Poland, would most likely carry the lot of us. Suddenly, therefore, everybody of English speech is discussing the right way to make war. The warmth of this sociable impulse is noticeable. We find ourselves able in conversation, after but little thought, and often abruptly without thought, to throw about armies, ships, and air fleets. An understanding of martial strategy and tactics appears to be common and intuitive, unlike geography and physics, which call for time and study. That our opinion of the proper ordering of battle is so firm occasions no surprise in our friends, who should know our capacity. This may be so because they also are talking, and do not seem to be paying proper attention to us.

War at least works this sprightliness in the mind. Though horrible, it wakes us up. It animates in a way good news finds more difficult. War, if sufficiently distant, inspires an onlooker with a sense of power. It quickens into eagerness for the mastery of the tempest even those not always sure, in easy days, of the train they ought to catch. Such episodes as Pearl Harbour and the loss of Singapore release our mental reserves. They disclose a fund of innate knowledge most newspaper readers were unaware they possessed till the prompting came, in a moment of time, to arraign Authority.

We may admit that Authority has blundered. That is not blasphemous. It has been ascertained that governors, generals, and admirals are no more infallible than postmen. Still, to be fair, we should also admit that to harmonize in an ocean the courses of the ships of a great fleet so that sufficient power can be at any point in the right hour is not a task for every man's delight. To dispatch armed men by land, sea, and air to meet a foe who has the choice of rendezvous, but has not named it, needs second sight and other uncommon supports to free the act of worry. To order off many choice men and much precious material on the strength of conjecture out of the measurement of facts that are not available, despite the awful consequence of error, error which the enemy has a mind to establish, is not a responsibility for which most of us would compete.

The other day—it was the day we heard that the Japanese irruption had covered Java—I listened while a group of eager and honest elderly folk were explaining it, or explaining it away. I was sitting in sad and silent remembrance of that lovely island. They were undecided whether the loss of Java was of first importance or of small importance. In the midst of the talk a spectacled and youthful corporal leaned towards me and murmured, "Our wearisome and pedantic art of war; By which we prove retreat may be success, Delay best speed; half loss, at times, whole gain." The corporal had been sitting back in self-effacement till that moment. All he had done was to glance at me questioningly once or twice. As he was so young I had supposed he felt merely humble while the experienced and judicious were engaged in settling the matter. Then, having quoted Browning to a stranger, he winked slowly, adjusted his glasses as if the wink had displaced them, and sank into nonentity. A cipher! That, of course, is what he was; let us ever bear that seriously in mind. A corporal does not count among the innumerable nobodies who are flung wholesale into desperate adventures to save by skill and courage, if that is possible—at times it has been impossible—whatever chance a situation offers to rescue a little of good, after the fallible sagacity of Authority has almost or quite lost it there.

I feel that but for these sparkles from younger people I should be inclined to wonder whether the light was going out.

But it is still there. It is only somewhat smothered by neglect. The signs that fire may be as positive in the secret heart as is spring in cold mud are so frequent that a day seems dead unless a chance aside like that by the corporal touches it up. A gay word, at a late hour, brings back the morning. We may confidently look for happy announcements not yet known at the broadcasting stations. These men and women are at present busy in the field of war, and driving the factories at high speed; but a day must come when their wit, quickened by attention to novelty, will sparkle unsubdued by the gravity of ancient institutions, by established usage, archives, and the frowns of grey-haired jurists. That is the hope which keeps some of us going. If it should reach fulfilment, then the loss of Singapore will be only a footnote to history to mark the end of much that was due for oblivion.

At times they provoke us with guesses at the probable origins of common disaster. They point to occasions in the past, which we had supposed were forgotten, when high judgment was drowsy, and they ask whether the elected intelligence which now sends them on perilous enterprises has much improved since then. One thing which interests the younger sort is the supposition that this war could have been stayed where its first shot was fired, in Manchuria. They do not accuse anybody. They are like Miss Dartle, and are merely curious. They suggest that the timidity with which we watched Japan's behaviour must have been noted thankfully by lawless men everywhere. It announced that anarchists were at liberty, if low cunning could keep a face of shy reasonableness long enough, to permeate everywhere for the undermining and ultimate downfall of civility. With just the sort of motive which prompts a man to save a neighbour's house when a blaze takes it, the free governments could have limited the fire in Asia; instead, it ran on to consume the world. The point where universal ruin began can be marked on the map; and that mark also shows where the spurt in the abundance of our taxation began.

A youthful corporal will suggest that though inactivity seems both cheap and prudent at the time when courage is called for, cowardice can be expensive and even fatal. That may be only the view of active youth. But, as we look back, we see that Manchuria was only China; yet what of the sequence, from Jehol to Shanghai, and south to Hong Kong, to Manila, Singapore, and Batavia? Yes, and shall we add from Madrid to Warsaw and Paris? There was a day when juristical non-interventionists—this too is an unlucky matter of history—would not allow the hospitals of the Spanish Republicans to have cotton-wool, though the Fascist powers were sending bombing squadrons to Spain. As Mark Twain once pointed out, how deadly is the silent lie! For which of us cried out? We remained dumb witnesses while Chinamen were killed and their goods stolen; and as the wounds were Spanish that had to be dressed with dirty bandages, we felt no hurt.

It might be as well to own up, since the future depends on the accuracy of our knowledge and the quality of our conviction. For we see now that if in the matter of the drains of their cities the peoples of the democracies had acted with no more good sense and humanity than they have shown in international affairs, then we should still be fighting typhus and cholera as well as the present enemies of the mind's sanity. Is it more immoral for the Japanese to be looting and killing in Singapore than in Nankin? It is no less wrong in Nankin than in San Francisco and Australia. All the peoples of the world are of one body. Prelates as well as poets have full authority for that dogma.

We are still appalled by what happens when nations run

amok, and we have trouble enough, but there is yet that other
enemy to bring to book. If reluctantly we look for him, another deplorable fact soon appears, hard to acknowledge; it
is always hard to admit failure, when that is personal. For is
it not ridiculous in a democrat to blame his government when
affairs go wrong? He is the government; or, if he is nothing
like it, that also is his affair. What is education for? Democracy
is the luxury of personal responsibility; and what is responsibility, if justice, through ignorance and neglect, is indistin-
guishable from wrong? It begins to look as if an enemy were
in the house. The democrat who loves liberty seems to have
been on easy terms with him. Anything to his personal advantage he claimed, but harm that left him untouched he did
not feel. When he heard of distant havoc he was seldom
curious enough to experience it in more than an atlas. He has
been heedless of the meaning of most of the scenes where
good has been outlawed in long years of foreign news. What
did not knock at his own door was not answered. Only this
day does he begin to remember, and fear drives him to a
general accusation that he may rid himself of dismay. He
blames this authority or that in his own country, or preferably
in some other country. The New Yorker, the Londoner, and
the Parisian are alike in that; it is human. Fear will make a
man suddenly and fiercely political while forgetful still of the
fact that he always was a social creature, but had forgotten
his neighbours. Explosions are lighting up those lands lately
of no interest to him, and the blasts shake his kitchen. But
were not geography and economics always such dull subjects?
Were not ideals always impracticable? Was it likely the men
of Palembang would bleed, if cut?

Today the relationship of Vladivostok and London, Paris
and New York, surprises him. It is disclosed, by a rain of fire,

that continents are not separate bodies, but areas of the round globe, which is small and sensitive. So an old question sounds a little plainer. Who is my neighbour? Whatever happens anywhere presently sends its impulse up the Thames. I learn that the way I regard Moscow means life or bullets to fine fellows I do not know. In the long history of mankind the day is here when we must accept the fellowship, or take the penalty for denial; and the lack of fellowship is death.

We did not want war, but it was supposed peace was able to look after itself. It was only the absence of war. There was nothing lovely in peace, nothing absolute, calling for vigilance to preserve it, nothing as real as market reports, which demand knowledge and attention. Peace was but a quiet space in which to do and say what we pleased. An unofficial Washington commentator remarked recently, "the concept of this war is British, and the British, strictly speaking, are not in the war." What sense of responsibility was at the back of that man's mind? Perhaps it would be better not to ask; but I will suggest that, until the guns went off, he had given small thought to what was likely to happen when war was not pedestrian, but went on wings and wheels; that he had never guessed the first explosion would shatter all the sound textbooks of war into broken words, and leave commanding officers without guidance, looking seven ways for inspiration. Yet that truth could have been found, after a brief search. The British concept of war! Was that shown at Dunkirk?

I suppose we had no clear concept at all except to hold on lest we be blown off. It would be safe and profitable to agree that not anywhere on earth, which brings in Germany and Japan, was there an admiral, general, or air-marshal who knew what would come of it when the new forces which science

had given them were released. Germany, at the outset, made
a pretty good guess, based chiefly on the moral disintegration
of France and hesitancy elsewhere; but the forces, as she understood them, are not at present working quite so well for
her. Japan looked on, reading the lessons, and profiting from
them in a way we have not; for our attention, with no en-
joyment in war, was apt to wander. Yet the lessons were all
new to Japan; there are her previous mistakes in China to
show it. If war is the last instrument applied to politics, then
not a politician or warrior anywhere seems to have known
how the instrument would certainly act, when applied. The
French General Staff, by all accounts, was absent in a fabulous garden listening to the cuckoo when the bugle sounded.
Mussolini did not distinguish between war and grand opera,
Hitler conceived an unheralded outburst of tanks and airplanes to overcome all at once, and the British had the ancient
concept to hold on and hit back when a chance came; and
presently Japan, too, will feel the embarrassment of the unexpected. The only statesman who seems to have judged fairly
well what might come about, and to have prepared for it, and
who had a body of people behind him resolved to act at the
call, was Stalin.

It is not great fun to admit these facts, but they will continue to exist. To abandon some pride and prejudice will
lighten the burden; there will be less on the march to cause
suspicion, doubt, and bickering. We need only remember that
in all the democracies the usual citizen was intent chiefly on
personal benefits within his reach. When he became grave
and important about liberty, that is all he meant. With eyes
bent narrowly on his interests he did not see the sword
dangling above his neck as another interest, and so never
paused to wonder on the chance of a squall, and from which

quarter, bringing that thing down to destroy him and his liberty.

And of course he was unaware that each new war confuses the venerated old brigade, infallible till the outbreak with the honours of historic campaigns. He did not know that the experienced paladins, after the opening phase of the tumult, would be getting back to school. It meant nothing to him that after the first months of the last war all the immense armies went to earth, and the generals knew no more what to do next, having no classical centre and flanks to pierce and turn, than a bust of Julius Caesar. Not that there is ever anything new in war but the weapons, but these may make a plan of campaign, in a week or so, about as applicable as an old newspaper. The machine-gun was master last time, sinking men into burrowing animals, till the tank, newly arrived, and four years of mud and lice, loosened a measure of mobility. The first apparent lesson of this war moving on wings and wheels is that an army's centre and flanks may be ignored altogether, and that it is fatal to go underground on the defensive while considering what to do next, since it is possible for the foe to speed right on to the seat of your government and occupy it. The enemy arrives not only by road, but by sky and sea. Soldiers who went to this war confident in the lessons of the last grand occasion were soon without flanks, centre, or base. They were surrounded.

The mistake they made was in not going back far enough for their lessons, not by many long centuries; but it is absurd to blame them, because only now do we see that the latest weapons have compelled a return to Red Indian strategy and tactics—another of the wonders of science—with all the oceans and continents in which a Daniel Boone may spring surprises; and nobody had thought of that. Quite the strangest outcome of total conflict with steel foundries, industrial plant, ships, broadcasting stations, the newspaper press, and armies that are winged and wheeled, is that, as in the days of chivalry and the battle-axe, individual wit and initiative have broken out of the academies, and are making light of the gravity of the whole pedantic art of war. The value of the person is restored. The conflict, too, is in the mind as well as on the gun sites.

But then war, though there is never anything new in it but the weapons, is paradoxical itself, and so rarely teaches us much. We desire, when the guns cease, to clear the mind at once of its ugly litter, and leave but the memory of comradeship. It is even paradoxical that we should recall but good in the hateful. That may explain why this war caught us once more. We had been inattentive, while badly disposed men were alert to the chance of gaining power by the extravagant use of new engines. They judged that the speed of motorized pill-boxes and of winged artillery ought to be good for a surprise, especially over the careless and reluctant. Yet those Panzer divisions, dive-bombers, and wheeled columns but recall what happened in Europe long ago, when Mongol archers, who were mounted, came from the steppes of Asia to sweep over armies of footmen with pikes, and occupied the centre of Europe. Nothing is new in it, except the last use of those expedients as old as arrow-heads, surprise and speed.

America is wondering, so we are told, what the British army is doing. As an old war-correspondent I know a word about that. By far the greater part of our army in France last time was raised in the British Isles, but outsiders never knew it. We never told them. There were numberless battalions of our county regiments, taking most of the casualties, yet they were rarely named. The censorship was shy over those common names. The British themselves were informed chiefly of the doings and valour of troops from overseas, and of a few favoured home regiments. We have nobody to blame but ourselves this time when other people wonder what our men are doing, since we prefer to praise men from the Dominions and India; and they have earned it, as the conquest of North-East Africa shows. Still, our own men, too, were there; though we at home were unaware of that till the casualty lists began to arrive. Presently we shall hail American prowess handsomely, but will be shaky and indecisive with the trumpet on our own account, through that nervous habit of understatement. Fearful of making too much of it, I have noticed that our soldiers themselves are immoderate in their moderation. When a bomber crew alighted recently, after a raid over Kiel, with their machine in tatters, and I asked how the wreckage had remained aloft, and on fire, one youngster answered that he didn't know, but he rather thought they were having a touch of luck. You can never get those fellows to talk. Ironic and allusive, all that happened was some luck, if they come through.

We learn with surprise, in a brief message, of an outbreak by one of our commandos; of ships, airplanes, paratroops, and infantry becoming one force in an adventure. Yet it is an event to meet one of those men. Where they are hidden and trained nobody seems to know; and they are as circumspect with us as though we were the enemy. But we do know their training would break the heart, if weakness were there, of a hardened explorer, for we have heard stories of it; and exploration, without regard to peril in unknown territory where they are not wanted, is their vocation. We are back in this war to first things. The heart and intelligence of the common man take on a significance that transcends the power of the

machines. The man himself is again of first importance, as in
the beginning. And nobody had thought of that, as another
outcome of war waged by engines. May we begin to hope that
Frankenstein will at last gain control of his monster? He knows
at least that the very devil is in it.

So strange a consequence is auspicious. We had forgotten,
even in the democracies, that the person is above the State and
its machinery. All its elaborate machinery, without his hap-
piness, is an offence that should be ended. His word sanctions
the State and gives it purpose, just as silence may give consent
to iniquity. That original fact has been obscured by the noise
and dust of factions contending, while the illusion of peace
allowed it, for the safeguarding of money; but now, since
society is threatened with anarchy, the common man is quicker
than the jurists to sense the peril, for he has no precedents but
the freedom of his thought, and the necessity of his hearth.
Out of imminent disaster comes the beginning of understanding. If the household and personality go, then nothing worth
having would be left, so he gives his full value to save the
rights of his neighbours. What more could he do?

We return to first things. It has been remarked—only by a
poet, I know, and not by a prudent measurer—that in the
familiar Hebrew description of the way Creation came about
the first prescription for darkness was Light. It is usual to
assume that this bright revealing of the task of shaping things
out of primordial night and confusion was by the heavenly
lamps we know. Not so, says the poet. Light came first. In the
only way a poet would understand creative effort, the sun
would have to be imaged before it could shine. There must be
vision, or a thing that is to be cannot be willed to arise. Light
was, before heaven was above or earth beneath; before the
sun rose, and moon and stars. Mind came, to prevail over con-

fusion in the universal dark. In the beginning was the word for order and comeliness. But darkness was not destroyed. There it still is; and the original creative word loses power when it is forgotten. Order and comeliness, though settled under the firmament, and seen to be good, have to be kept, or disorder and darkness flood in to founder the gains. Creation never ends.

V

Wreckage at Sunrise

JUNE 1942. The prospect from London Bridge is not what it was. The mute appeal of ruin is disturbing. In a cold light one sees in a glance that in war the guidance for a good life must be reversed. To show generosity in war might set your town alight; and havoc no sane man would think of, especially at sunrise, takes its infernal place as a benediction in death's new way to success. The worst becomes the best. For our gift of reason, which places us above the beasts, can justify, according to the way things are, every variation in all conceivable desires, as though devilry could juggle unseen with our soundest argument. What tiger would sink into prolonged and careful study, and then give himself to rigorous training, that he might enter another den with the least risk to kill his neighbour's cubs? Tigers are not known to do this. Simple ferocity is deficient in intellectual planning.

Despite the assurances of the Church and the academies, we should not accept too confidently the story of our superiority to the beasts. That unique ability to think things out is dubious. We are beginning to see that the best of intentions followed in flawless logic may take us anywhere but to the desired haven. So odd an outcome of man's special privilege, that the conclusion to an argument for prosperity can be in hell, appears to carry a further warning. It would be prudent to assume, apparently, as the saints have told us, that man's supreme gift is not from blind chance and for no purpose whatever. But suppose he did get it that way?

No, we will not. We dare not. As some security for the continuance of hearth and home, let us firmly believe that in such an idea hope dies for want of air. That supposition is nihilism and old night. There is a wide choice for the use of the mind, but let one purpose remain above all others, the ageless search for truth amid the mystery of existence, and from this search it is better to exclude self as much as we can. Self, we have sad cause to know, is unsympathetic in this greatest of adventures.

The mystery is excessively darkened at this moment, a consequence of man's efforts to improve his place in the universe. There the wreckage is. He has been far too clever. To put things right again, we are called upon to destroy instead of create, and we obey without misgiving. There is no misgiving because our way of life, and the institutions of our choice, without which we feel existence could have hardly any meaning, have been marked for burial, and the last rite has come so near that we have had to stare Death in the eye, waiting for his stroke, for a period which felt like a century. It is not enjoyable. But in the meantime, we cannot help noting, the moral order we are defending has become as reproachful as a policeman's helmet in the gutter the morning after a riot. The symbol of law and order is soddened and battered. This unsought trifle of observation, while we still actively dodge explosions, while trying to save the altar, is startling in its mild reminder of sanity in neglect.

It is as if we were warned that sanity, which we had almost forgotten, is still somewhere in the background of our affairs, waiting for the passing of the gun-wheels. Just for an instant we surmise that those wheels cannot be endlessly turning; a calm morning will come, with no ships blowing up, and no houses on fire. Only the silent ruins will be there, waiting for a re-creative word. And then?

Well, one begins to wonder already whether the primitive surge of passion necessary for the defeat of an enemy who would abolish us may be no simple force. It may carry us beyond our aim, and we not know it. It may have unsuspected attributes. Its logic may take us far astray, and lose us. There was a book, written soon after the end of the other war, by a brave soldier and thinker, and its author, C. E. Montague, called it *Disenchantment*. What disenchanted my friend Montague was the continuing hateful look of the world when he had put up his sword, his enemy being down and out. Do you remember, too, the valorous warrior in the old fairy-tale? He was a good man, but his aim became impure in his pursuit of a monster, and thus it happened that when at last his cunning shaft transfixed the brute, and he was victorious, he saw that he had also struck his love in the heart, and his world in victory turned desolate.

How much more confident we should feel in battle if we knew that, in the welcome dayspring of peace, we did not in victory look round on desolation, with beauty dead in it! Even now, while we watch the enemy for the first signs of his downfall, a doubt takes us of our liability in victory. The gravity of the matter begins to be felt when we know that the English-speaking peoples are chiefly responsible for the future welfare of mankind. That is our fate. If we refuse it, our fate will be no better. Though whether we have the good will for the task, and sufficient knowledge for it—have we so much as the knowledge? You have but to listen to the voices clamouring around to guess that Peace and her dove, when they arrive, if welcomed by common passions, might show only a few scattered feathers by next morning. It will be far easier to win the war, though that has looked impossible on some days, than to save the peace.

The worst thing in the shouting and the confusion is the suggestion, as though we were haunted, of ghostly sounds heard out of that other war; menacing echoes, well remembered, from behind the years. Those disenchanting noises grow more familiar and more insistent as the gunfire and alarms of this war increase. You say it is mere fancy? That all in those years is dead? Yes, it is certain our friends are dead, those gallant hearts who stood to it in the old front line, with only a clear conviction, and no heat, and no hate. The echoes are not of their battle-cries, for they never exhausted their souls with hate. But voices from that half-forgotten war we certainly hear; and they are older even than that, and reach us from a past still more remote. They are as old as humanity; as old as cruelty, and as recent as rage this morning over frustration and loss.

The fierce excitement which confuses past and present is becoming the war's most alarming problem. How if, when we have victory, we have our worst selves to fight? Barbarism not only quickens its own sort, but can make barbarians of us all. The Nazis, desperate through fear, are murdering innocents and old people, thinking to rouse a general terror which will preserve them when they turn their backs. Their loutish ignorance is unaware of the power of the army of the dead. Dead men tell no tales? Do they not! What a tale these dead men are telling! The spilled blood of innocents is more terrible than heavy batteries. The memory of the martyred is in the very grass and stones, and follows the retreating feet of executioners.

Some hostages are shot; and free in that place from possible danger, the Nazis march to another village, to do the like. A huddle of unknown men and women lies against a wall, and the quicklime is sent for, to end the matter. But the matter is not ended. Phantoms have been called up which guns cannot manage. Horror, hate, vengeance, fury, the hosts of the pit, take the place of the villagers, and thus it is our lot to fight, not only evildoers, but malevolence they have released universally from the dark of the mind. How did each of us feel when news came of what happened at Lidice? Yet, with such news, we are expected to be rather better than Cromwell's Ironsides, who were not surprised and changed by anything; as good at least as George Washington himself, who had occasions to be indignant, but did not lose his head. These atrocities, in truth, force us to battle with ourselves, and for that secret warfare there is no practical manual, no guidance at all but one's own candlelight kept by what faith one can muster in the best message, known to us all, ever vouchsafed to wayward man.

The clamour of the multitude is not easily resisted when it comes of revolt against cruelty and loathing of bestiality, for it is a generous emotion. But it is only an emotion. Resist it we must, for our purpose in this war is superior to all transient gusts of the feelings. The foundations of an international commonwealth, as free as is possible of the motives which have made Pandemonium the newest and most appropriate name for Earth, would be ruined by stains of hate. Resistance to wrong counsel will come easier when we remember, amid the tumult, that common people everywhere, whatever their colour and nation, are friendly to the friendly, prefer good neighbours to bad, and life to death. Our foes are the men who have our fellows in their power. To break the power to control the lives and opinions of our neighbours, whoever has it, is our sole excuse for taking to the gun, though that argument was forced on us.

It says something for democracy that its chosen leaders in this revolution are men so superior to their opponents, in most that makes men great, that we are as grateful as though we had been given a sign. Roosevelt, from London to China, for one, is heard because the right word tells as surely as daylight; his counsel creates a good spirit where the immediate prospect is without hope. But we should fail, nevertheless, if we depended only on our leaders. Amid the clamouring of the multitude we catch the right accent at times, and know that the nobodies could not have chosen such leaders if unaware of the virtues. I heard, recently, an unnamed British airman broadcasting. His aeroplane, he told us, was one of a flight of fighters which chanced on thirteen German air transports over the sea, flying troops to Libya. He related how they shot down eleven of them: "An airman's dream come true." Following a giant plane down to the water, to make sure of it, he saw what happened when its company was cast into waves alight with flaming oil. That young man's voice fell. It was clear he meant to tell us more, but he faltered, and said simply, "It wasn't good to see." He then went off the air.

And a soldier home on leave—he was through the Battle of London—was with me on the Sunday morning when it was announced that more than a thousand planes had bombed Cologne. He put his hand on me, as if for support. Later, thinking it over, he recalled the argument which the Fascists had started, and confessed that it was our hard luck to show them what its conclusion must be. There was no other way. Still, he was affected. Londoners, I think, regretted the cruel logic of it. They knew what it meant. They themselves had suffered, in their minds, bodies, and homes.

Amid the uproar, one meets persons who speak as citizens

of the world. They keep, in chaos, their sense of individual responsibility; and certainly without that understanding of
civility even a democracy would die. The great city is the city
of the best men and women. Its rulers cannot make it great. If
the right spirit is not in its tenements, then the city is as dead as
ashes, or deserves to be. And if ever there was a day in the
story of humanity when the common man must summon his
wit and will to decide which way history shall go, it is now.
All depends on him. Unless that fellow chooses to refashion
this earth nearer to the heart's desire, our communities must
perish. The danger is, not that he is unworthy and unwilling
to choose, but that he has never understood history to be but
the story of himself, and from as far back as the day when
his weapons were stones. History is, in all its lessons, no more
than the imperfect reflection of his apprehension of good
and evil.

"O, Sairey, Sairey," Mrs. Harris once repined to Mrs.
Gamp, "little do we know what lies before us." But Mrs.
Gamp, having no reason at the moment to be cautious, remembered simply that she had had to be a mother more than
once, and said to her friend, "Not much, it's true, but more
than you suppoge."

Mrs. Gamp's speech, as a rule, roved in attractive guile
while dodging its subject, but for once, concerning the shape
of things to come, she was more honest than nicer people
often are when accounting for trouble. She knew what to expect, when aware of a cause for it. No romantic secret was
made of destiny and its inscrutability; no sorrow, as with noble
minds, over man as the helpless sport of the gods. She didn't
know much about the future, but she could not pretend to be
non-contributory and in complete ignorance of what was in
store.

Shall we, too, own up? Because more often than we are

willing to admit—there are pride, prejudice, and perhaps investments, to be preserved—what lies before us must be the result of what lies behind us. War, like plague, has an ancestry. Even peace, when we see it, will have features resembling whatever is present in our minds this hour. What is it we are thinking? Could not forethought work good into it, as well as the satisfaction of hate, and improved bombers? We have seen how battle tests the virtues in men and their societies, and that lofty bunkum and clever subterfuge have not the survival value of dirt. This suggests it would be better not to pretend that we had no part in generating folly's progeny; that their real father was Fate. It is clear that man may dispense with the help of Norns and Fates. I have but to look on ruin in London, remember what has happened to this planet since the use of metals was discovered, and name the successful creature who did it all, to understand that man has nothing to learn from the Furies. If he is a little lower than the angels, he is also, when he tries, the most ferocious and destructive beast that ever lived.

General tribulation does not fall from the blue uninvited. We have known for some time that it is more expedient to examine the drains than to attribute epidemics to witchcraft. Destiny is but the last refuge of fools who could have known better, and acted more decorously, but discovered too late they were woefully out in their reckoning. The common defects in humanity, which are such splendid fun in satire, are enough to account for history's black chapters and our present desolation. There is no need to add the further hopeless idea of an Immanent Will which does not care what happens to us. Let us, since we are forced, admit the truth of it: as we are, so is our world. How much does that leave Fate to do with the future? After all, our understanding of the problem of living was slighter than our churches, libraries, laboratories, and universities suggested. Enough knowledge was possessed to have crowned a civilization, but good intent would not appear to have gone far enough to correct perversion by cleverness and greed.

Has there ever been a grave upset in social relations, such as this blasting spectacle we now watch to see whose house will next catch fire, that has not had its origin in plain sight for years, to those with eyes? It is already an old tale when the man in the street, casual and unlucky fellow, stares in dismay at the announcing headlines. Too late! He affects the innocence of a child in a street accident. He is unaware that he has been inattentive, for he could easily have known that this was on its way to run into him, unless he and his neighbours gave it urgent thought, and balked it. Too late now! There is nothing for it but the recruiting office, or the bankruptcy court, or both; both, usually, being in the same street.

It was written of the Treaty of Versailles at the time it was published, "This is a bridge of tinder over hell." If you would learn what the rosy confidence of proud man can be when he is most sure of his brains, and at a turning-point in history which would have sent archangels hurrying back to the empyrean anxious for further advice, go to the records of what public men in Europe and America were saying and doing for ten years following November 11, 1918. On the other hand, don't. It might make you ill. But I was a journalist then, and for long after, and was compelled to suffer it.

As to Hitler and a number of others, if we knew the millstones were about their necks, and at this moment they were dropping into the midst of the sea, tonight would be calm and starry. But our greater problems would still be here. Hitler is incidental, not a cause but an issue, like the outcome of neglect when the human swarms are disorderly. We should never have heard of him in a world that had been sanely active. In May 1919 I was editing the London *Nation* in H. W. Massingham's absence. One press day the text of the Peace Treaty came in. The journal was nearly done, but that emergency had to be examined and given first place. Then J. A. Hobson appeared in my room, the most welcome man in England. He was not heard to enter at any time; he had the approach of a wraith. I thrust the document at him gladly, for a first perusal.

All serious students of society and its ways have heard of Hobson, and they may care to know that Lenin, to his confessed advantage, had read that Englishman's works. J. A. Hobson was the most selfless, learned, and wise politician and economist I have known. His tall attenuated figure stood at a reading-desk that day for an hour, without a movement, except to turn another page of the document tenderly. He had an air of arrested venerability. He was aged, but would not grow older. His dry and drab exterior would remain unchanged by weather and circumstance, on the point of extinction, but constant. I remember him with care, because, though he has really gone, his quality is with us, and could help. His sparse and grizzled hair and moustache were untidy. He would have been quite neutral but for his eyes, which had a dancing glint. That sign of vigilance was most of the liveliness his body showed, except that, when he was stirred, one eyebrow rose, a warning to the clever ones that they were seen through, if they cared to notice it. One of life's pleasures has been to watch that eyebrow go up, and an admonitory index finger rise with it, at the end of a loud debate, when Hobson's sly fun and better knowledge kindly lowered us to ground level. At length he turned from the desk, looked at me over the top of his steel-rimmed spectacles, and used his index finger on the document for punctuation. He said, "This is a political and military document. It means bayonets, not bread. It took four years to win the war. It will take forty to win the peace."

Though more than half that period has gone, we are still hard at it. There can be no single and simple reason for this long unkindness of Fate. It is not in nature that troubles so protracted, involved, and severe should fall on innocents from an ever-vengeful sky, or humanity would have died out before it had reached the ability and leisure to improve the grape and make music. Nor could those frustrations have come from the diabolism of a few evil men, however powerful. There is no easy absolution for us. Our activities must have been wrongly inspired. What intelligent man would care to swear his country's past is like the virgin cheer of Eden? He remembers there is the evidence of history.

History is not bunk, as a famous and pious industrialist once said, perhaps hoping to exorcise some effects he disliked by denying all cause. It is history when children's teeth are set on edge because their fathers ate sour grapes. Because of law, we look to harvest beyond the sowing; and as to one crop, whatsoever statesmen sow, that we must reap. Every country has its lively variety of politicians, which makes it difficult for one nation to be solely responsible for universal woe. Some countries, usually small, have long outgrown the desire for aggressive war; and some greater nations have become weary of the glory of trumpets and drums. We may fairly say of the American and British peoples that they regard war with dislike. But aversion from trouble does not keep it away.

Let us recall that, during the last war, we became so numbed by years of concussions that when the uproar stopped we were only glad. Our grateful apathy was the opportunity, golden of course, for men of energy and cunning whose interest in personal advantage remained unimpaired and close. The abrupt and welcome end of the war, and the following inconsequence of populations tired in body and will, was the chance for those who represented conventional ideas and aims, out of which the disastrous conflict had arisen, to slip back into the seats of power. This they did, unrecognized for what they represented. And there, in control, they were, during all the years when naked swords were beginning again to peep through the soil. Our chosen leaders ignored the phenomenon. We may only surmise that among the general ideas which govern the policies of industry, commerce, and finance, not a notion was to be found for controlling and extinguishing the glitter of lethal steel, when its sharp points began to spike up once more in the fields of earth, superior to corn.

Not an idea to promote a purpose so good seems to burn brightly with those whose thoughts are fixed on personal advantage. But it is for ideas we are at war, since we have been forced to declare that we would sooner perish than allow the best that humanity has won to be lost in ultimate night. We will not taunt those politicians and publicists who could not find, in the years behind us, time to attend to ideas, and to discern the difference between black and white, but we may point to the fact that they could have read Hitler's testament. They should have noticed that such infectious stuff out of fevered lunacy, which could not have gone far in a land where print was free to all and purchase optional, was imposed as holy writ on the folk of a great country; a nation always strangely submissive to harness, curiously willing to obey orders contrary to its own repute for scholarship, thought, and art, to ignore its sentiment for religion, and to march in a tranced state, it never knows where, to it doesn't know what. The voice

enjoyed its liberty. That liberty can be had but at a price; a price men may be reluctant to pay, I suppose, even for residence within the jurisdiction of Zion. They are slow to give up anything, even the causes of their tribulations. What, give up the satisfaction of hate? There can be nothing remotely resembling a city ruled in wisdom while citizens are slow to surrender self, and to surrender it for no more, in return, than the privilege of serving. The desire for mastership is difficult to forget, though the vast majority of those who seek mastery usually find themselves, in the long run, on the dole, or in a worse place. It is not so easy as it seems to give our best to society instead of our worst, for our existence is suffered by our neighbours not on the highest terms, but the lowest. This is obvious even in the arts, and in politics it is notorious.

If signs are to be found for a way through chaos, we should begin somewhere near that admission. Any effort seen anywhere, in one's own community or outside it, to control the right to live and serve where there is liberty, equality, and fraternity—values not in the foundations of any city ever built —should be dealt with shortly, as the police handle a malefactor breaking the peace. It should be so highly unprofitable to assume a claim to mastership that men would as soon choose to be lepers. But education for that has hardly begun. The schools are not built. No church is here yet. The pioneers are but surveying the wilderness, and the only faint promise is an Atlantic Charter. The capitals of the world have arisen out of blind life lusty for power, and now they are threatened with decay. Material welfare in its greatest display depends on the sanctions of the host of nobodies, and when those sanctions are withdrawn from the historic prospect of ships, harbours, spires, warehouses, and factories, that show of rich reality proves to have no better roots than the famous hanging gardens of Babylon.

Those gardens have perished. And the magnificent efflores-
cence of this age of machines, young and freely budding as it
is, spreading wild everywhere till of late, may die off; for the
winds of doctrine are not easily forecasted, and they blow now
from a wintry quarter, bad for all human interests subject to
rust. The latest work of our hands is not only more delicate,
but requires justification from which gardens are exempt.
The admired wheels, without they have good reason, may
cease to turn. They got their form and use from the motives
of this age, the spirit of our time; but that inspiration was
always ambiguous, and religion and the arts have been shy of
it, on instinct, when not deriding it. The poets have always
damned it. To attempt to justify industrial civilization with
the plea that it works, while we witness it in dissolution because of its inherent falsities, would be stupid. Great cities
have the aspect of the desert. Our democratic institutions,
with no more to keep them going than their old inspiration,
will fall, and our forums and schools revert to thistles and
chance weeds in emptiness. In Europe already the weeds are
in possession of the brickbats; we look around, and there the
sterility of our former brave notions faces us.

What then? As to failure, we may cheerfully own to that,
in a new light, while there is freedom to begin from a better
mark. There are other worlds. There have been signs for years
that the spirit of man was ready for new and greater adventures. The oceans and continents are explored. Material
conquest can go no farther, except to the conquest of itself.
The breath of life is stirring anew. Man's apprehension of
circumstance is widening. The possible is enlarged. We have
glimpses of space exacting greater faith and courage to explore
than were needed for the circumnavigation of the earth. We
start from here. It is another day, and we have struck tents and
are on the march.

VI

Salute to Adventurers

DECEMBER 1942. I scan the headlines of the news and then try to read between the lines; as likely a way as there is for an approach to the truth in news of continuous war. Reading so, I often fancy a shake of anxiety in a simple message from a Washington correspondent. His duty is to report the latest, but he seems worried lest, meanwhile, I develop a dubious notion of America; or else should trust her too much—it is sometimes hard to tell which. He fears that while he informs me of progress towards victory, my sense of being an ally may faint. Probably he remembers that most of us know just where peace went astray last time. It was when Americans walked out of the League of Nations.

This anxiety is noticeable in correspondents resident on the west side of the Atlantic. They doubt my will and capacity to understand a scene treacherously resembling the English. They keep hinting at the existence, where they are, of an historic prejudice, at times flamboyant in its suspicions, and of tastes and opinions to puzzle Pall Mall, and of literary divergences very confusing to a Paternoster Row that was; of a foreign scene, in fact, deceptive through its superficial likeness, and further perplexed by the requirements of political hocus, and of worse motives, better not described. Therefore please make allowances. For aren't we all in a fix? And in battle, how suspicion of the friend at one's back would boggle the sword!

It would. And I know of a peril far worse, and it could arise with victory, should mistrust separate comrades. Triumph would not be Nike, but Medusa.

It was with such a thought that I heard, quite appropriately, the wailing note. The enemy was on his way. I went out to see what I could. It was night; and sometimes a blackout must be groped into, to be believed. No moon and a low sky made a London suburb Plutonian. I seemed to have gone blind, and the silence was of that ultimate deep which life has never reached, where day has never been. Then a searchlight shot up a bright beam to splash on the ceiling. Others joined it. I was indeed alive, and could now see there was still a sky, because explosives were suspected to be roving in it. There it was, our world without light except that of hell, shaped by clever men with reason and knowledge, and as void of excellence as a cannibal bone heap.

Indoors again, to await what might come, I did not select but picked up—modernists may laugh if they feel like it—a volume of Emerson's *Journals,* and retired into the 1850's. Strangely, I felt at ease in New England of those years. Nothing was there to upset my prejudices. It was home. No suspicion arose. Emerson could have been present talking easily across the hearth. He had a joke or two. He mentioned Carlyle as if he had just left that fellow round the corner. Is there a faculty in a man which indisputably marks his superiority? I think it is prescience. He made me jump once, when he suggested dirigible balloons, and a great war to come that, for a change, would be for ideas. He was as much a contemporary as this week's Washington correspondent. He did not, however, entertain a suspicion of the man to whom he was assessing affairs across the hearth and the years. I felt no isolation. He appeared to know me quite well. Where the two of us met, we had not to reckon time and space, so had no reason to fear this and that.

If understanding can be as easy and pleasant as laughter, not subject to geography and the gap of a century, at the same time—we had better confess it—suspicion and prejudice, the outcome of ignorance, have the same advantage. They are as perennial and ubiquitous as blue-bottle flies. We have to bear in mind that hate and bigotry are older than the Pyramids. Nor are they local. They ought not to surprise us anywhere, not in the American Boston or the English Cambridge less than in Sokoto. Men everywhere are affected by the peculiar advantages of birth and customary association. None of us is greatly helped by a bias of education which ignores or under-values things and forces that are beyond the village. There is another difficulty. Though false values and crooked measures are worse than ignorance, yet they can assume dogmatic authority; they have sent good men to the gallows.

Still, ruin is educational. It provokes us into seeking a cause, and that is a bit to the good. And a renewal of education, surprising in the gladness of initiates, is beginning to vivify curiosity and to raise a ruthless questioning throughout the world. One reads of coolies in Chungking who drop their loads to spell out, on a hoarding, news of New York and London. Danger overcomes prejudice quite easily, and will increase a desire for better knowledge into anxiety. I have found myself on a long railway journey this winter exchanging news with an American soldier from the Middle West—he had never been overseas before, and New York was strange to him —as though our tokens for values had similar imprints. It please dhim to find that he had been misinformed about us. His only remaining dislike was for the English climate, if we had one. I could see he was no foreigner to a woman opposite, whose husband was missing after Dunkirk, for when she told us why she believed her man was alive, after over two years' silence, the American gently encouraged her hope, which was more than I could do.

And a friend of mine, navigating officer in a ship of the convoy which took American troops to North Africa, was gratified to find young foreign soldiers come crowding to the forecastle at night to get lessons on the stars, and how to use them for bearings. He remarked that he began on his guard with them, and they with him. Starlight united them. He told me he laughed sadly when the landings began. The Americans seemed eager to be away to a party; but they were off an African beach which he had reason to dislike.

I wonder how many Americans knew of Guadalcanal, Macassar, and Akyab when the alarm came? Perhaps as many as the English who had no need to consult an atlas. It is probable that most members of the British Parliament, despite the suspicion of their leaven of imperialism, would succeed not really brilliantly in a test of their knowledge of the history, geography, and communications of British Dominions and Colonies. When Malaya came into the news, Penang and Pahang would have sounded much alike to a fair number of our legislators. Some of these reject the word "empire" for its ancient and forbidding smell. Other members, to the eyes of youthful and ribald critics, seem to be but Victorian monuments dedicated to the memory of Clive, "the boy who won India for England."

Obsolete monuments we may disregard except as warnings of what critics in a time not come may think of us; but, since Clive is named, a little of the history of eighteenth-century India, to discover the kind of difficulty which Clive had to manage, would be helpful. So would be the admission that

Robert Clive, whatever we may think of imperialism, personified the very qualities which have made America great. While considering what we had better do after the war is won, it would be useful to have the past in just perspective; otherwise it will be difficult to discover where we start from.

It is remembered, even at Westminster, when Penang and Singapore are mentioned, what kind of men were Francis Light and Stamford Raffles, officers of the forgotten East India Company? Raffles, who founded Singapore on a few fishers' huts, went to Java to protect and govern it when Napoleon occupied the Netherlands, and he established a tolerable rule which the Hollanders have developed. Imperialism may have what import a critic chooses for it—and should he desire it, I think I could supply him with arguments to arraign it; but that would still leave Raffles a beneficent and enlightened figure in a barbaric world, a man who gained nothing even from his own people for his selfless service, except the usual neglect and grief. In truth, the company of explorers, navigators, missionaries, and administrators, who have gone from England, under various impulses, to discover, settle, establish law, and rule, have had among them not a few of the finest minds in Christendom. While dismissing ideas repugnant to us, we should not dismiss facts, though they seem opposed to an idea we prefer to entertain. A certain amount of tolerance is helpful. Mistrust can end in bigotry. Consider the regard for truth of a Nazi judge trying a Jew! The trouble is, though we would search out the truth in a matter, persuasion comes only through knowledge gained by patience and honesty, whereas to damn offhand saves time and requires no thought.

The spirit of man, our special care in this war for ideas, is, as Wordsworth regretted, a pure flame but early in life. Things so soon happen to the tender child. There is his home, the mythology of his neighbourhood, and the good or ill luck attending his labours, all going to his education. He is too intricate a creature for us to compel into wisdom, though we had it to offer, as though he were a horse simply obstinate over our pail of pure and kindly refreshment.

Could we not begin on the rights, prejudices, and privileges of our country by declining to examine too strictly its frontiers? Where, after all, does America end? Where England? Suppose I wish to claim Roosevelt to be also my President in some important particulars? Suppose my neighbour prefer Stalin? If we should certainly look twice at gifts some foreigners may offer, at the same time Wendell Willkie is nearer the heart of many of us than not a few of our own earnest exponents of what is and what should be. A man can represent values that are acceptable anywhere on earth. Does equity vary? To whom do religion, poetry, and music belong? If they possess us, they are ours. What is a foreigner? It depends on what the man is. I could name a Chinese or two more like home to me than patches of the local directory. I suspect I should be as well understood in Chungking as in some circles in London.

There is nothing esoteric in this. It is not peculiar, like those passwords, or catchwords, which sadly exclude many of us from certain select centres of intellectual interest. This sense of fellowship is usual in the cinemas, where war workers go for entertainment. Russian pictures bring instant applause, sincere and perhaps intimidating. The records of the Chinese confirm kinship. The cause which has brought the United States, China, Russia, and Great Britain together, to most ordinary men and women, has the urge of religion, and is limitless in its scope. Its inherency is indefinable and dangerous. Generous aspiration always leaves the question of personal safety to the last. This quickening of charity for one's neighbours has been enlarged into human life. A common relationship has been found, and no narrow interests can stem its power, though they will try. Some of our leaders know this; others do not, though they will learn.

This is new in politics, but it is not new in history, though the signs of it have received less sympathetic attention from historians than other human wonders. All the founders of the world's religions were aware of this attribute latent in the spirit of man. It abides in stillness till it hears the word it will understand but does not know. Once, in Paris—how many Americans are aware of this?—Woodrow Wilson could have evoked this power, at least in Europe. It became clear to the innumerable unimportant, as they caught rumours of what the peacemakers at the council table were up to, that the war was lost to them; that they were to be left in the past. Dismay was universal in the mean streets and byways of a continent. The nobodies waited expectant for a word of hope, which did not come. It was their trusted politicians they heard speaking, and hope was not in the official agenda. For a brief hour, as it were—not for much longer did the opportunity last—if Woodrow Wilson had made the magnanimous gesture at that conference, had he addressed himself beyond the restrictive chamber to the unseen multitude, with the call for which it waited, Europe would have risen; but he was unaware. Then apathy and the shadow fell over all. We are involved in the consequences.

That cannot happen again? Of course it can, unless makers of mischief find their business has become unsafe and unprofitable. They may find it so. It happens that this time the nobodies are not only expectant, but reliable bodies of them everywhere are resolved. For this time the word has been spoken, and there is a common will to let the dead past bury its errors. Attempts to re-establish those ways of national life which led to this catastrophe may, we hope, find ignorance not so gainful as formerly.

As there is no return, except to the ruins and the bones, had we not better go forward? It seems the only rational act. It is therefore a grave matter that misgiving in Washington over the honesty of friends, unlike that doubt felt by a naval officer for the American lads in a transport, has not yet been cleared in the light of the stars. Is Christian faith worthless in foreign relations? It has never been tried, but some way must be found to overcome those fears which always exist between men when they find themselves joined by chance in an adventurous quest, desperate with perils, and to an end unknown. It is open country ahead of us now; and if comrades fail each other there, then they may abandon hope. There is no alternative between anarchy and law. I do not wish to contemplate an earth on which reason and good will are dying out.

We know, regretfully, there has been nervousness over recent radio atmospherics caused, among other things, by a suspicion of imperialism and its subtle aims. But it is all to the good. Let the air over the Atlantic crackle! I feel free to touch this matter because, in the long ago, I was called, with some others, pro-Boer. I am still that. It can be fairly claimed that England is the world's traditional anvil on which political theory is hammered out; and the sparks fly. Ask General Smuts, of South Africa. He is a philosopher, and one of the best of living statesmen, and he knows, for there was a year when he was our implacable enemy. Yet we had a far-seeing and generous Prime Minister a few years after the Boer War, Campbell-Bannerman, whose memory should be honoured, and Smuts was brought over to us. When I am challenged about my imperial bent I waste no time. I point to Smuts, and

leave it to him. Whom he cannot convince there is no con-
vincing. Then again, could an American Colonist have pleaded
with more fervour for his freedom to choose than did Lord
Chatham on his behalf at Westminster? That historic fact is
in the English tradition; the same tradition which put the
English with their backs to the wall, resolved to have it out
there or perish, when Hitler had subjected Europe. A new
political dispensation, monstrous to them, was threatened, and
they preferred to be dead rather than accept it.

British legislators may know far less than one would have
expected of the geography, communications, and history of
their dependent Colonies and independent Dominions, yet
about political theory the British in general have always been
as various, lively, and exploring as those original Athenians
who were very curious about the how and why of things. The
historic sense, without much particular knowledge, was always
exciting in our little islands. At any time, when form is being
given to government, trouble may be expected. Privileges and
ancient rites, however attractive, come to be seen through, and
are challenged. Even our kings have had sad cause to know
that. The culture in which the English work and brood has
been in secure continuous life for so long that its inheritors
trust to its general trend, and do not concern themselves with
particulars till time and chance tell us we must move on.

Yet we ought not to expect other people, among them the
people of India, to be aware of this; and it cannot be denied
that to many of us India is a fairy-tale told by Kipling. But
who knows enough of India to be confident? India, unlike
China, has not a fairly homogeneous culture. It is richer in its
variety than any other area of earth that could be named. The
stage in its evolution reached since Clive's victory at Plassey is
not to be discovered in a speech or a leading article, however

eloquent. That subcontinent of many languages and religions, with its incoherent story going back near to Genesis, is a problem of government not to be solved emotionally, and in a grand rush. Are not four hundred millions of people concerned? And besides princes, politicians, mahatmas and gurus, wealthy merchants and manufacturers, landowners and money-lenders, there are peasants, factory-workers, and a class in its hierarchy called "untouchables."

India must be free! Yes; and the Sudras? Will they be free too, as free as the upper castes? When India is enabled to make its own political decisions, and that will soon come about—there is no other meaning to the fuss—will the peasant get enough to eat? Some of the native states are still round about the fifteenth century; and at the same time an Indian may think what he likes though hungry, and worship what suits him. It seems to me that while poor men anywhere are unsure of sufficient millet, rice, or bread, there is a deal of cant in this talk of political freedom. I should guess for the Indian ryot it will not mean a damned thing. I should say for the Bombay factory-worker it will do nothing to reduce overcrowding and its incidental diseases and death-rate.

We forget that never anywhere has there existed a right democracy. It is a form of government still in the experimental stages, and of interest mainly in the Anglo-Saxon communities. We overlook this, though the shocking spectacle of democratic and republican France ought to be warning enough to scare the most noble patriot from pursuing his political ambition till it end gloriously in what he wants, or in the dismay of his people. It is taking us much too long to learn that politics and finance are two aspects of the same thing. Gandhi knows more of India than it is possible for us to learn, and, probably, of other important matters; but, when he saw invasion threatened across Asia, and divined that all he had to do was to persuade the Japanese to give up war, leave China, and go away, what help was there in that flash from his insight? And why should he wait for the Japanese to invade India before dissuading them from continuing destruction, loot, rape, and murder in China? Couldn't he have saved China before this, if aware of the right method? It seems such a pity to wait. While reflecting on these mysteries of constructive thought, let us recall that nearly all India's many millions are poor men, peasants and workers, who do not know much, not even why it is advantageous for a few other men, white or brown, to control their lowly way of life.

The very magnitude and urgency of a problem will drive us to dismiss it in impatience. To win better knowledge takes time and thought, while pious and emotional incantations can be immediate. Nevertheless, we are fairly sure that India is ripe for change; our empire, we are also vaguely aware, was always subject to the principle of life. We have even grown shy of the word "empire" of late years, and the obstinate use of it today by a politician arouses wariness. It is preferable not only to say "commonwealth," but to realize, as well as possible, its implications. We are on the way, but have some distance to go.

India is named, not to excuse white rule in Asia, nothing like that, but as a warning of what there will be to do, when a chance comes to compose the complaints of peace. The Russians also are in Asia; and beyond India are Burma, Malaya, Indo-China, and Indonesia. It would take the bulk of the Atlantic to accommodate the East Indian Archipelago, where the Dutch used to rule. Several of those islands, Borneo, Sumatra, and New Guinea, are great countries. Java has the area of Eire, with Javanese, Arabs, and Chinese among its peoples; and Celebes is somewhat larger than Java; and the smaller isles are like the stars in multitude. Malaya itself is not a simple piece. It has a mixed population, negroid nomadic dwarfs in its mountain forests, Malays, various Indians, and a great number of Chinese.

Can that continental region govern itself? Not if peace and plenty are looked for. We might as well leave the Japanese in possession. Chaos would be a mild name for the outcome of an experiment there in self-government. Self-government needs aptitude, and education, and a long patience with disappointments. As the Americans and the British themselves are but in the shaky early process of giving form and life to the principles of democracy, it would be wrong to leave the many peoples of that spacious region, resigned to fate when under the age-long tyrannies of numerous native chiefs, to the designs of the kind of energetic men who would certainly shape our own destinies, if we were ignorant and indolent enough to let them do it.

We hardly know yet to what this war commits us; we are only beginning to surmise it. There is—or there was—the trifling item of the British occupation of Hong Kong. We had been there a century when the Japanese took it over. Doubtless we brought fertility, engineering, and profit, to what was only a barren rock, but our original lien, to my mind, won't bear looking at. It is possible to suppose, however, that the Republic of China, when guns cease to have an immediate function, may desire that Hong Kong should be, for a spell at least, a haven for friendly ships. The Chinese may not wish their allies to leave their coasts on the day that guns may be neglected. The spoils out there are such a splendid attraction.

The work before us when destruction ends and creation should begin will daunt anyone who would prefer ease and comfort in a return to his accustomed occasions. He will get no comfort from those occasions; they will have suffered a change. The morning when the storm is past will not seem so gloriously bright. That morning will see emerge from their hiding places too many desires and fears; the fear of change felt by the timid, the hostility of men of great possessions who fear to lose a chance for greater, the fears of the hunters of place and fortune, of those to whom profit is above service, of those with minds devoutly set; of all to whom ideas are never right when new. We must expect, in fact, an attempt to stampede us in dread back to what we knew for safety, in the name of individual enterprise, and for God's sake, and for every reason that blood-shot rhetoric can imagine; but what we knew will have gone, quite gone.

There will be no safety but in the acceptance of danger. It is useless to bargain with life; one must take it as it is, to do the best with it. But I believe that, dark as the morning after the storm will be, yet the youthful in mind will be aware that "only that day dawns to which we are awake." They will be awake, knowing it is day, and will be ready to share with strangers the fullness of life in a new age. Their thoughts will expand to the occasion, and be out of bounds. National frontiers to them will have lost the old meanings. They will strive to release human relations from constricting bonds, to free the bounty of earth for the use of all. The world will be ready again for the enterprise of adventuring minds. Its seas and lands are all discovered and explored, but the best use to make of them is still undiscovered. That is yet to be found. Pioneers have to learn how far the spirit of man can travel towards making a garden of his place. I do not see why Christians should fear an attempt to establish the Kingdom of God.

Man cannot live by bread alone, we know, and his condition remains unimproved by luxuries; but he cannot live without it. And bread has always been chancy for too great a number of people. An uncertainty about tomorrow's loaf will distract a man's attention from the truth that he is spirit as well as body. Is there much freedom for the spirit when the body's only liberty is to get through to tomorrow, if desperation can find a way? We don't know what dimensions of the soul are still unknown to us, undivulged in unemployment statistics, cast out in the slag-heaps of our activities.

When respectworthy democrats are proud of their country's institutions, and wish others to share these benefits, it is only freedom they are thinking of. The benefit of individual liberty includes the right to starve. But political and religious freedom are not enough. What, freedom to fight for the means to eat and breathe? When harvests are destroyed, so that prices may be maintained because prices are more sacred than homes, the scramble of the lord of creation for his food is enough to make the lower animals laugh. It looks then as if man were more like the fool of creation.

When this war began, about two millions of our neighbours were unemployed. I have been told that America had a few. I don't know how political economy explains or excuses this waste of power and wealth, and I don't want to hear. It is wrong, that is all. It is wrong. It hurts the mind merely to be aware of such a fact; and to look into the eyes of a child condemned to hunger and withheld from joy is to know that civilization is a falsity, whatever the late architecture of its institutions. Let us cease to lie to each other about hunger and the restriction of life in a disguising scientific jargon. That is what we have been doing, and libraries are full of the clever evasions of the scholarly. But hunger is hunger, dirt is dirt, ignorance is savagery, and hopelessness is death.

As to the future political administration of those lands at
present given to war and anarchy, unless Americans agree to
keep their minds clear and their coats off for the demands of
peace as they are doing for war, anarchy, more or less, will
abide, there and elsewhere. We need be in no doubt about
that. You might as well, after great risk and labour, get a
drowning man ashore and then leave him unconscious to
perish on the beach. And reviving him and setting him on his
feet will not be enough, this time. We are bound, by the look
of it, to enlarge the family, though he be an Indian, a Chinese,
or an African.

Personally, I like the look of it. I wish I were young again.
The Renaissance from the Middle Ages was nothing to this
uprising in the Industrial Era, an era which was past its time
and dead, though all speed, smoke, and uproar. Long words
have been used of the needs of the world after the war, poly-
syllables as callous to human warmth as abstractions usually
are. International Political Control! That is, the use of common sense so that such a disaster as this cannot again burst
open our isolation with bombs. And Economic Co-operation!
The wonder is, in an age of machines which made more than
we could use, that we had to wait for universal bloodshed
before discovering there were myriads of people who were in
need of food and shelter. It never occurred to us that bayonets
always go with trade barriers; there is no other way to keep
those barriers shut.

And who benefited? Not the producers, not the consumers;
not, that is to say, most of us. That lesson for us is clear enough
in Hitler's own avowed intent, which we mean to thwart. His
sole aim was the economic lordship of the earth. That was
what he was after from the start. His assumption of political
control, with secret police and agents to keep it, was but a

means to that end; he knew that political power without the prize of earth's riches is meaningless. His tanks and war-planes but issued in logic, and there they are yet.

They will be removed from daylight presently, and the way open again. It will not remain open for long. Let us carefully note the significant instance of Admiral Darlan. Will it help if many of our avowed enemies come over in victory to guide us? We had better know beforehand where we want to go. We might, while in a state of elation, be hurried off in the wrong direction after all. It is certain the right way will not long be free, after the guns cease. It was shut last time, and not by accident, before the soldiers had buried their dead. If this war does not release man's spirit to the noblest venture in exploration of his existence, then we fail. It is no good talking. If the war does not bring us to unity in the cause of all mankind, then it is lost, and we are wasting life and treasure. We have never had that fellowship, though for two thousand years there has been a promise of it. In the light of what we have learned in agony, shall we ignore the gate, since destiny, or Providence, opens it for our choice?

VII

The Ordinary Fellow

MAY 1943. A neighbouring coastal town had a visit yesterday
from the enemy. This war is "global," a word which puts it
with the hallowed abstractions, a zodiacal affair, so the official
account of some blasting done to the eighteenth-century houses
and shops of an obscure British town was necessarily brief and
vague. "Yesterday morning three enemy aircraft dropped
bombs at a place on the South Coast. Some damage was done,
and some casualties have been reported." That is all the
people who were not there, the global host, were told. More
could not have improved their knowledge.

A few of us were less fortunate, for we could supplement
the official bulletin, but did not feel like it. We felt instead
that complete ignorance of some happenings is preferable to
exact knowledge. For this reason, when as neighbours we met
again, our exchange of news was laconic and ambiguous. The
truth is, when bombs and cannon-shells are aimed from a low
level at a provincial High Street, in the hour when women are
thinking of war in terms of rations and coupons, you are unable to say much about it, though you were there. What
prevents you is not the strictness of the official censor. You are
prevented by that censor everybody acknowledges when ruling
out anatomical particulars, human and exposed. War is ob-
scenity so foul that its facts choke utterance. We can but stare
numbed at what we see, as if speech were not fashioned for
this.

We dismissed the subject of yesterday's irruption. It was not our first shake-up, but one is always free to hope it is the last. Thus we hoped. The following silence, while we gazed at the fire, was broken by a young woman. She remarked reminiscently, "You know, as far back as I can remember, all the news of the world I've ever heard has been bad." There was a hint of reproach in her manner, as if we had deliberately cheated her of good tidings.

We turned to her. What she had said was, in its way, more startling than the raid. After all, we have gained the point when we merely note the warning siren, trust the brutes are not heading straight for us, and get on with some work; and our trust has been falsified often enough to make the consequences of bombing, unless personal, worth but allusive comment. For war, when at a safe remove, is always an impersonal abstraction, as various and entangling as metaphysics or the marvels of the subconscious. Like the problem of pain, war has a perennial general attraction, but to this attraction its sufferers are listless. But this young commentator had pointed to a matter rather more serious than war in our street. Humanity, she complained, had never provided her with good tidings. Could a young, healthy, well-educated, and pretty woman say anything worse of the world?

She must have supposed our silence meant disapproval of her youthful opinion, though of course it meant merely that we were not ready with some clever jugglery with history as we preferred to read it. Because then, with the coolness of a statistician putting social morality into the exactitude of numerals, she explained that one of her earliest recollections was of resisting her mother when being taken from bed down to the coal-cellar. But mother stood no nonsense; down she went. By candlelight, while her parents sat on the floor listen-

ing, the booming of guns was very sad. It was like the barking
of a lot of big dogs. It was a Zeppelin night. They often had
one. A smash of glass still frightened her. She then went on
to give us a casual selection from the news of many nations
since the 'twenties.

What of general good, she asked, could we set against that
uproar? A few books and poems, and the excellence of or-
chestras? Little more, she thought, except the work of phy-
sicians and surgeons, aided by pharmaceutical chemists and
research workers; nothing whatever from religion, and not
enough from any source to prevent serious people from speculating on how long it would be before the ground gave way
under us all.

At last it gave way, and nobody with a pennyworth of wit
expected anything else. Since the other war, the drift of things
had caused young people, her generation, to suppose that, in
a world of lies and calculated selfishness, whatever one did
was of no particular significance, for there was no universal
law, and no authority worth respectful acknowledgment. If,
she said, divine law and authority were mentioned, young
people merely wanted to know why God allowed evil to do so
well. And that ended their curiosity in the question. They
expected no answer, and got none. She paused for a moment,
and then said irrelevantly that last week the earth, almost
overnight, changed from drab to green, and yesterday she saw
the first swallow. She informed us that there were early cow-
slips by the copse under the hill. It was lovely, yet she felt
there was no time to be glad. She had got into the habit of
waiting for the next shock, so even spring sunshine seemed to
be in a place apart, and not for her. "How can I be grateful
for spring, when people who know more than I do tell me it
is the season for great offensives—always has been?"

When afterwards I reported her to an elderly man of religion, he was silent for a while, and then said her indictment was not only just, but the responsibility was his; and that others, if they felt like it, could share the blame. And what ought we to do? Because, he remarked, if the earth continues to be such a place for the young that its beauty is meaningless to them, if the earth is to remain a place where it is difficult to rejoice, even over the first swallow, then God's purpose is lost.

He admitted, before we parted, that he himself gave up, became resigned to the dust of a confusion he guessed would grow worse, a month after the last war ended. "What could I do," he asked, "after it was plain, as it was by then, that all the lofty sentiments expressed by statesmen, all the promises made to keep the common man going at an awful job, were to be thrown out for burial with the dead? Statecraft, on behalf of money and privilege, and afraid of losing control of the inadequate machinery of government, which it didn't want to improve, played upon the weariness and heart-burning of the multitude, following four years of agony, to conjure itself back to power.

"What could I do? In my church, I felt like the psalmist, who was required by the Babylonians to sing them songs of Zion. I hadn't the heart for it. Yes, I'm afraid I resigned myself to captivity. All I did was to maintain a ritual faithfully. That girl convicts me and my generation."

A time has come, and we are doing in it as well as we can, which is called the day of the common man. We cannot help noticing that most broadcasts are addressed to that fellow. Suddenly he has been promoted, if not to nobility, then to indispensability, thus ranking above earls. There is an unmistakable note of anxiety in the appeals to him to sacrifice himself. For him propaganda is designed, as if nothing could go right unless he believed with all his heart that our intent is just, and for his good. The microphone might as well be a flat-iron if he were not listening. Without his approval, the news agencies and the newspaper press could be devoted to skipping-rope, or anything you please. If the queues of him dwindled, the film studios would realize a worse thing than war.

So he has been lifted up. This is his day. Nothing has really happened, of course, nothing new, except that it has dawned on us, if dimly, that the State, without the hearty singing of the national anthem by the nobodies, would be a legend and a silence, like the stones of Nineveh. There can be no doubt that when a country is threatened, then, unless the nobodies save it, it is lost.

At the end of the other war, when the nobodies, by pro-digious exertions, and sacrifices too awful to contemplate then or now, succeeded in their effort, and cleared a space in which we could breathe at ease again, and were free to rediscover the use of reason, they uttered no complaint; they did not even pause to see whether their names appeared in the list of honours and rewards, but hurried away down their byways and side-turnings, to count what bread was left in their cup-boards. This could not have taken them long, but they did not show up again prominently till they were told that all they had done hitherto to save us was undone, and now they must do it again, for their very lives. What is all this fuss about a Beveridge Report? The very necessity for it condemns us.

There are intellectual aristocrats who shudder at the thought of the common man. That he should be honoured with a day takes importance from their own existence. He is a rude creature of appetites but no taste; body but not mind. Some-

how, they do not know how, he goes on living without resource to what, for them, are the founts of life, about which,
showing as it were in Pierian grass, are the imprints of the
winged horse; or some other token of original authority in
perpetuity.

What he does not know puts him in a sphere with which
they cannot communicate. There the language they use says
nothing. He can but build and drive a locomotive, or a ship,
or judge when to plough and sow, or moil at a coke oven. He
has never so much as heard of the Upanishads, Virgil, the
Early Fathers, the Encyclopedists, the Impressionists, and what
not. He has not begun. His rough surface is inappropriate to
drawing-rooms, where, after all, the allusions in conversation
would be less obvious to him than a dropped plate. He does not
care for poetry, except when he understands it, and he would
die miserably if left alone in a Celtic Twilight. And when,
hopefully and experimentally, the new movements in art and
music are tried on him, he seems puzzled. The latest artists
and writers, with their new apprehensions, are wasted on him.
He has never read Marx or Pareto, and would not understand
them if he did; yet it is known that the Parables of Jesus reach
him with the ease of sunshine. How does that happen? Does
it mean anything?

To bother us still more—for certainly this fellow is a problem to which we must give a little attention—it has been discovered of late years that he can be almost as attentive to
Beethoven and Mozart, and even to Bach, as he has always
been to Handel, which makes it harder than it used to be for
critics of fine discernment to dismiss Handel with his popu-
larity. But even the recent news that at times he responds to
the music of the privileged does not bring him closer to the
intellectuals and refiners, who remain aloof, distressed by his

incuriosity for the qualities which give them their peculiar
significance, and by his gothic humour and his earthiness,
which come of his coarse labours on the line of subsistence; and
he has such simple desires, satisfied mainly with the luck, if his
luck runs to it, of home, leisure, and games.

He is "the mob." It was the mob, we remember, still perplexed, which was the fabulous public of Dickens, a fact which
does not impress the intellectuals, as Dickens was a barbarian;
so, for that matter, was Shakespeare. It was the mob which
once trudged to the Crystal Palace during the Handel festivals.
But that is not the worst of it, not by a long way. The mob,
though enormous, is not only difficult to make out, but it has
latent attributes which to some people are terrifying.

One notices this when reading that scholarly humanist, Dr.
Inge. The mob frightens him. Yet it is easy to sympathize with
him, and to feel a tremor of his alarm. A familiar study, and
Plato in use, ought to be not only quiet but immune from
rude disturbance and change; the only intrusion of noise from
without should be the rooks cawing home at sundown at the
end of another day of peace. It is unsettling, while watching
rooks in immemorial trees, with the tower of a fourteenth-
century church in view, to remember that the spirit of man
is unrestful, and bloweth where it listeth.

The common man, the mob, is unpredictable. He is an un-
shapen and dubious form of life, and very numerous. His emo-
tions are not only stirred and gladdened by good music and
certain gracious words. As the unforeseen rising of the wind,
in which establishments topple that cannot face tempest, the
human spirit—moved by God knows what—can enlarge into
an elemental and irresistible power. It is said the disastrous
Napoleonic era began in no more than empty bellies after
hope was dead, which seems miraculous. Where this spirit is

concerned, all we can do is to look for the impossible, and the impossible happened in China recently, and also in Russia. To have been in England during 1940 is to have learned something of it.

We are not helped when told that most of the famous historical uproars breaking the quiet of a reasonable existence came usually of stupidity so evident that correction could have been made in one move, if made in time; and after warnings that no dumb animal would have disregarded. We know it. Man is the only animal to accumulate knowledge, and to reason on its benefits, and the only one to make a fool of itself of choice. There are years, as at present, when one could suppose he is bent on making his existence an abiding horror.

Great upsets, we know, have come of black ignorance in high places which could have been cured by raising the blind and letting in daylight. Surveying general ruin, we see that all that was wanted to save it was a touch of good sense, not quite so much pride, and a little self-reproach. That is all. If only the few people who had common welfare in their hands had felt kindness before the sun went down! If only enough decency and gumption had been in high council to utter reconciling and creative words just not too late, then how much the less of woe!

That view of history, very likely, is illusory. Statesmen, though as great as Hitler imagines himself to be, are rarely of that stature, meek in nobility. The sense of power exalts into a form of lunacy called pride, which withers all it looks at. The worship of great men, and other myths, comes of common human yearning for an authority above its own modest capacity, which it feels to be inadequate before the unpredictability of existence. And then, too, that spell-binding drama of the last days of an international crisis, when the red spectre looms, is deceptive; as we watch the going and coming of inimical messengers we are fascinated and appalled, and reason leaves us. We are unable to think.

The solemn figures in the drama, whose speech and movements hold us, as if we saw the Norns in a dire twilight working out our fate, are in reality but speaking their parts, making predestined moves. This drama was written for them long ago. They are compelled by the past. The tragedy they enact till the light goes out is of the long play through unconsidered years of the ordinary thoughts and deeds of men, and of their negligence. This is only the last scene. This is the meaning of it all. The bias to catastrophe was formed long before by prevailing notions and common mental indolence, though its purport was not manifest till the hour when society began to topple over, for at last our eyes were opened, but in dismay. Says Ecclesiastes, "That which hath been is now; and that which is to be hath already been; and God requireth that which is past."

If we had to instance this, almost any page of history would do. A story goes that once that wise American Thomas Jefferson proposed to a Congressional committee that, after the year 1800, there should be no more slavery, and he was defeated by one vote. One vote! And then, perhaps, that little debate over, and its decision registered, the committee looked out the window, and wondered whether it was going to rain.

One vote! But is not regret misplaced? That vote mirrored Jefferson's contemporaries. They were like that. He himself had not, perhaps, divined the way things might go, but he hated every form of tyranny, the use of force for personal motives. He knew that kindness is not in whips, and that society has no security without the sense of fellowship. His mind was superior and prescient, but his advice was given to the wilder-

ness. The people about him were unaware there was much to
question, except the usual hindrances to private fortune. His
judgments had no reference to the land they knew, which was
not a wilderness, but the commonplace of home and effort.
Jefferson was, in fact, not there with them, but distant in
another time. That is why he was aware the confidence his
friends reposed in the continuity of their daily scene was given
to a slowly dissolving appearance.

But how tell them that? How choose words as concrete as
a pioneer's axe? He was aware that the thoughts of men,
which shape their world, change as their perception grows of
a moral order informing the material universe; and how explain that, to make it as plain as a crucifix? For their part, his
fellows respected him as a good man—though he had odd
views, which were harmless, because not at all relevant to
things as they were.

The truth of the matter, we may fairly venture, is that
when our country fares ill, each one of us must answer for it.
An inheritor of an estate takes over its mortgage. He ought
to know for what he is responsible. But if in careless freedom
he is interested in only the gossip of the day, and himself? If
what was laid up for him before he came into possession, keep-
sakes and remembrances not always suitable to lavender, put
by last year, and in years before that, if these things do not
engage him, because other things make better fun?

Well, at long last he is awakened. There is a knock at his
door. It is the State. He is ordered to submit and render. He
was unaware he was in for this; but who is to blame? For he
is the State. The State is men and women, ourselves and our
neighbours. Without individual conscience, the State is no
more worthy of affection than a temporary erection of scaffold-
ing; than a system of sanitation; than any other convenience

compelled by communal life. To make a god of it, as some
people do, is to add another devil to the world. The State is
us and our goings-on, continuing what our fathers did. For so
just a reason, that young lady, a child when the last war
began, who remarked that all the news she had ever heard of
the world was bad—though she named a few exceptions—
was not far out. Her accusation points at each of us.

The business of men, after the last war ended, would hardly
bear looking at, if one began to think it over. Most of us have
heard that said, or something like it. And there was no escape
from it, as monasteries had long since gone out of fashion,
though the daily scene became more and more strident, coarse,
and violent. The headlines in the press, you will recall, were
not only like echoes of cries from Pandemonium, but were
never sufficiently sustained for common expectancy; there had
to be wild inventions. The craving for excitement suggested
that to be febrile and convulsive proved that life was good.
Even the arts were affected, as was natural, for they must
reflect their hour, which was hard, harsh, noisy, and dis-
ordered.

That quickened rhythm of life! It ought to have warned
a casual onlooker that society was out of heart. What society
worth the name could there be when it was speeding nobody
knew where or why, with no direction and no bearings; no
time for anybody to stop, look, and listen; to say nothing of
considering the lilies of the field? It was as if all were hurrying
to escape their own shadows, a life of desperation in a flight
from discontent, which clung to their heels.

There was no more a central conviction upon which society
could remain steadfast, no Athena, no Apollo, no Zoroaster
or Confucius, and the authority of our own religion, once
absolute, had been taken over by science. Bethlehem, and the

homage of wise men as well as of shepherds, had gone. For a substitute we turned to the physical laboratory, and believed in measurements instead of beatitudes. It is simpler to work to a formula, when one is hurried and has no time to consider ease of life; besides, what can graciousness do to increase the power and load of the engines?

Never in history has humanity possessed so great a body of knowledge for its use as we have today. With our formulas we have gone far, we can boast, and do boast, in the conquest of nature; and what has happened in consequence? Look around at our triumph! What we need is a salt to save us from the smell of this corruption.

Only yesterday I read in a sober and admirable London newspaper the assurance that, looking beyond this war, our technicians are working famously "towards the final conquest of the sky." Its final subjugation? Poor old throne of God! We shall upset it yet, doing as well as this. We are getting on. Already many of the cities of the world, among them some of the most ancient establishments of urbanity, have lapsed into desert. The rubble of universities, libraries, museums, art galleries, transport systems, hospitals, theatres, the memorials of celebrated men, and venerated temples, flourishes as thistles and ragwort. The seeking of impersonal truth has had to be changed into a fight on one's own doorstep with a legion of lies we thought had disappeared from daylight for ever. Pity itself, without which men are savages, has been forced to improvise means to rescue populations in extremity; too often these must perish in lands we cannot enter.

There it is. Our late wonderful accessions to knowledge have had their part in this; but was it supposed that forces by which we could, in a large measure, overcome space and time, alter the balance of nature, and bring either a greater fullness of life, or death, could be used outside a moral order, as though no more were involved than in a game of chance? The devices the laboratories and the technicians worked out to increase our physical abilities have brought about a holocaust of the innocents.

Then let us ask, if shyly, "Is it possible the empyrean has an answer to its conquest? May we not be looking at another glorious illusion?" Perhaps we should not be too confident that our success in releasing powers latent in the universities is all to our advantage, and to be used as we please. As far as our definitions of constructive principles go, they may be technically right; but they cannot be absolutes. They cannot be.

Then with what powers have we still to reckon, our knowledge? Perhaps they are for ever outside the reach of human wit. There are laws not embodied in our statutes, and energies undescribed in our encyclopedias. Truths we do not know may be enough to turn our glorious conquest of nature into arctic darkness and frost. While we stand before our achievements in admiration, even in adoration as they revolve to further conquests, perhaps a little compunction stealing over us might prove fortunate. Mercy came to the scene when the Garden was left, and we don't want to lose both.

The chief sufferer from the consequences of ambitious authority and cunning is the common man. As I write, I hear machine-guns going it in the blue. He is in the sky now, the ordinary fellow, and on such a fine day, in continuance of whatever designs we down below have upon the earth. And, if beyond that, the common man, who must win this war and another peace, can be quickened to the challenge that his also must be the greater part in ordering our affairs to a better purpose, then to me it seems impossible that he could make a worse mess of it than has been made by selected and dedicated specialists. It is not more knowledge that is wanted—there exists a mass of knowledge so great that the right use of it is blacked out—but good sense. If a superior and respected neighbour has all knowledge, and all wisdom, and understands all mysteries, and has not charity enough to see that we have not long to stay, and that we all go the same way home, and shall be on the level when we reach it, then it would be better to depend for counsel on the house dog, who at least can bark his sympathetic understanding.

We know of the injunction, when the matter is of first importance, to speak in the vulgar tongue, that all may understand; and the need was never greater than now for good speakers to have sufficient vulgarity to reach the outer fringes of the multitude with an urgent message. It is easy to fall into a hopeless view of human nature. That can come of daily contacts, with the pricking of envy and pride, and rejection through antipathy. We don't like the fellow, and he is met at every turn. To look out, when low and depressed, on the usual activities of mankind, is to see but a confusion of clumsy feet undirected by much of a head and by no heart at all, and heedless of the beauty of gardens.

That is always the early impression of the general scene, and to some despairing souls the view never changes. They can find no promise of a fairer time, when each shall be for all, and all for each. They cannot help remarking that the person, whose freedom we desire, so often uses it, when it is his, to sadden daylight.

With more experience, and with some sympathy for those innumerable fellow-creatures insufficiently gifted with the charm of egotism, one discovered that self-love appears to be the chief motive of men only because its effects are obvious, for they are irksome. What is distasteful is always sooner remarked than what is modest. In fact, not everybody is selfish. There are others. There must be very many others. Does not the world continue regularly to turn, in its common and uncomplaining way, war or no war, reward or none? These others are not importunate. They are never eloquent, except dumbly. They are never in the forefront; they do not resist when pushed more to the back, nor even when at last they are pushed right out, being old. They do not grieve over their lot, so we seldom realize they are there; the world merely goes on turning. They accept stony ground, where nothing much grows, as the only kind of earth that was made, and there they are. They are the great body of the folk, in which daily heroism goes unrecorded because it belongs to this way of living, and there is nothing to say. These people are a chief element in the landscape, with trees and grass, which we scarcely notice, yet should surely miss, if one morning we looked out and saw only earth's dry bones. The world would cease to go round.

After I have read dismal reports by health and medical officers, and have listened to the confidences of social workers, not always suitable for print, and so get the idea that civilization can include horrors that would be absent from a Hottentot village, I recall what used to be known as the "distressed areas" of England. That euphemism softened the truth to the comfortable that people there were dying slowly. They had not even hope.

I remember in particular one distressed Welsh mining town, which had the look of a community crumbling after a disaster, never to be set straight again. A man stood at a street corner, to whom I spoke. He was spruce and upright, but his clothes were thin and threadbare on a cold day. He was haggard but stern, and his grey eyes met mine as if he were a master of his craft, though now he did not practise it. I wanted to know how long he had been out of work. He held up three fingers. "Months?" I asked. "Years," he said. That sort of fellow, now proving his mettle in Italy, as he did before at Ypres, was one of the victims of the social lie with the fine name "economic necessity." Let us clear our cities of that before we ever complain again of barbarity in our midst.

In Tolstoy's wise book, called the greatest novel ever written —whatever that may mean—we can fancy we find a special affection of the author for two characters, General Kutuzov and the peasant-soldier Karataev. Both were natural men. I suppose most of us have met them some time or other. The general, though a courtier, thought as little of elaborate plans of campaign as he did of court gossip. He would be pensive while listening to a staff discussing the science and art of warfare, and then go to sleep while the talk went on, for he knew what ought to be done, but knew that Emperors would not have it so. He did not blink at the splendour of Napoleon, and was undisturbed by the magical success of genius on the field of battle. Prestige to him was a noise. He would listen as long as he could to an energetic dispute as to whether a battle ended in victory or defeat, and then doze off. He was aware that victory, strangely, can be disaster for the victors.

He retired from the field of Borodino, beyond Moscow, and guessed well what had happened that fateful day, though nobody else seemed to know. It was supposed this was another defeat, and Mother Moscow was at the enemy's mercy; yet his men remained confident, as if the sun and the seasons were with their general, and they could wait. Kutuzov perceived the drift of things about him, for he felt, being kind, what was undivulged in the nature of man, what was potent for good around him, and knew it could not be hurried, any more than spring in the course of time, and took advantage of his instinct to the undoing of the triumphant invader. He did not expect applause, nor look for honours. He had good sense. He did not hate Napoleon, but he had an idea that that man, now with glory about him, would soon be eating horseflesh. And who was he to interfere with the march of necessity, beyond the duty to move along with it, as his hour struck?

When the peasant Karataev appears in the novel, after a sentence or two we attend to this supposed simpleton somewhat puzzled, as if here a chance were offered to get an indirection out of innocence, greatly to our advantage, if we could fathom the drift of it, and could follow it in accord. We shall hear a word from this soldier, very likely, not to be found in the library, except also by chance, in the right hour, when one's mind is clear.

But Karataev does not know he has anything to say; he is friendly, and enjoys talking to another man. He is pleased to give himself. Life has been this way for him, he tells us, and laughs. He might be talking to his dog in solitude about the wonders of the road. He is as guileless as morning light, and when he laughs you can believe the fount of life flows clear at its source. And where is that? And what did he find there, and keep, that we lost long ago, and have never missed till this moment? Something has gone from us, though this man has it as naturally as breathing.

Both these men are as usual in the world as trees and grass. They are rarely obvious, and then only by accident. It is in our extremity that they appear, and to our aid. If we want to know the quality of human nature, let us search there, and not in statistics, and in the various salons and institutions, nor in the counsels of those with interests to serve. Hooker tells us, "For as much as we are not by ourselves sufficient to furnish ourselves with competent store of things needful for such a life as our nature doth desire, a life fit for the dignity of men, therefore to supply these defects and imperfections which are in us living singly and solely by ourselves, we are naturally induced to seek communion and fellowship with others."

We have heard often enough, since Hooker's time, that such an ideal is as attractive but as useless as the beauty of the Gospels, for human nature is against it, and human nature cannot be changed. As to whether our nature is changeable or not, one would give much to hear the view of a Stone Age man after a glance at a university don. Anyhow, whenever the likelihood is expressed of a fairer and kindlier time, there they always are, they who have interests to serve, or perhaps with no more than minds they cannot alter, facing us with their doleful bogy, and reminding us of the worst. We mean well, but they can give us no hope. What we desire is not within the power of human nature to bring about. Men never will voluntarily give up their possessions and their rights. It never has been done, and it never will be done.

But it is always being done. The critics have not been sufficiently observant. It is being done this day by the nobodies everywhere. Men have voluntarily given up the promise of youth, home, wife, children, wealth, and ambition, to further an idea of good for the world, which they may not live to share. Is that not also human nature? Is it not an advance on the Stone Age, and the stock market?

Human nature remains a mystery, and what can be conjured from it to the common good is at least as well worth trying as an attempt to disintegrate the atom. Let us attempt something towards the integration of the virtues in our neighbours. That, if successful, would provide us with power beyond the scope of shattered atoms. Abiding in the human spirit is a force which can be evoked to either good or evil. A word will move it. We have witnessed the miracle. Men are indeed born again, and their neighbours scarcely know them. Though we can estimate accurately the strength of expanding gases and of electricity, we are ignorant of the lift in human nature itself, when quickened by its ghostly endowment.

VIII

Night Watch

NOVEMBER 1943. Two American editors, their periodicals famous, are here to discover how things are with us. They have been to see me about it. But what could I say? For if a visitor should attempt a picture of England now, somehow to give it the right light, what could he do? I do not know, but I can feel sorry for him. If he knew us in past years well enough to be at his ease here, so much the worse for him.

He would be found speculating, I fancy, at the end of a week with us, whether all he saw and heard had a significance undivulged; whether there was a secret England, not yet disclosed; and whether he would live long enough to find it. With luck he might remember, to his enlightenment and solace, that that is the way revolutions always are.

Yet there certainly are some things in our background simple enough to be sure of; he could take them without question. They are as firmly fixed as his own belief that life, as well as we know, is preferable to death. He would find everywhere, even among the younger men whose lot is the hazards of battle, no doubt that to begin war is an insane act, and that corruption must follow it, but that armed conflict with the ideas Germany loosed at us was fated. The doom of this generation, and of the traditions in which it was born, was an article of Nazi faith. The gun had to be taken, unless we all agreed to have our brains dried up or knocked out.

Nor will a visitor have to ask twice whether it is known in

England that Japan exists, though the chances are he will not hear Singapore mentioned. We find that word not easy to say. But Australia exists; and then again, China is a word that means here what Russia means, and the man who speaks grudgingly of Russia is suspected by most of us to be a warped fellow, if not a probable enemy. Still, the fire is not out next door yet; the party wall remains red-hot. Though a visitor to London, whatever his doubt or his previous suspicion, asks no question about that; the smoke gets up his nose. Contact with a harsh fact is a persuasive argument.

An American, strolling about London, glad to see its streets again, seeking familiar haunts that have either vanished or are unrecognizable, probably gets the impression that the British metropolis, despite the defeat of Hitler's war-planes, is occupied by an invading army after all. It is a cosmopolitan army, to be sure, but in the main American. It must surprise him that Londoners are either unaware of this clear confirmation of Goebbels's prophecy of American dominion over the British, or else are taking the occupation as their due share in the re-ordering of mankind's business. In truth, it does not matter which. It is too late to scare us with that stuff.

We are in the mood to accept anything, if it means concord; any dispensation from men of understanding to get release from a nightmare which has lasted ten years. The continuance of Valkyries and other ugly monsters of Teutonic dreaming becomes boring and exhausting. Nor can we help speculating still, in a quiet spell, about the fate of those trainloads of Jewish infants moved out of France long ago, without identification papers. To where, and to what? Black instances like that occur to us of something unnamable at large, and enough of them in number and hideous implication to reduce the Newgate Calendar to the mild reports of a philanthropic society.

It is not surprising that an American should fail to find his London. I cannot find mine, and have given up hope—if hope is the right word—of seeing it again. It has gone. There is only a simulacrum to warn one that cities, like men, suffer change, and are mortal. Though we did not know it, because its presence apparently was as constant as the morning train, our accustomed city has been a view dissolving since we came into it. A city is but the shadows cast by men's thoughts, which are subject to time and the sun. What informs London now? Out of what desires will its future towers grow?

One can only say that the fine ideas in various charters, policies, and agreements, subscribed to by presidents and premiers, and in this promising plan and the other, are not gaily blossoming in London's vacant lots, and make no bright eyes in the daily hurry along the pavements. If you mention these spacious notions before young people, as assurance of future good, and compensations for sacrifice, the usual response is a faint smile and a cold silence. They do not altogether believe. This is a disillusioned generation.

T. E. Lawrence voiced their doubts for them in his *Seven Pillars of Wisdom:* "When we achieved and the new world dawned, the old men came out again and took from us our victory, and remade it in the likeness of the former world they knew. Youth could win, but had not learned to keep, and was pitiably weak against age. We stammered that we had worked for a new heaven and a new earth, and they thanked us kindly, and made their peace."

That scepticism shows also in sporadic labour troubles. Though miners and shipwrights are not unsocial, they have bitter memories. Everybody knows that between industrial combines and workers there is enmity, and that war never does much to turn it to graciousness. I don't think it is higher wages these workers want, though that is what they ask for; what they really lack is faith in the golden words of statesmen, which have been known to prove spurious.

Is this year's coinage of bright currency also of base metal? They cannot be sure that the alchemy of politics will not again turn precious words into dross. All they do know is that, while labouring to drive Germany back into her place, with Japan to follow, no light task, they see at home influential men, no longer afraid that Hitler will soon cross the Channel, coming out boldly into daylight and, to prove that fear has left them, freely talking from the dark of history with the emphasis of the industrial captains of the 1840's, when *laissez-faire* was the soothing remedy prescribed for the natural outcome of commercial and industrial anarchy.

This cynicism over the good intent of statesmen, a common human failing, is no more than faith defamed and mocked long ago by that government of men of business—for so they called themselves—which secured control at Westminster when the last war ended, and through ignorance lost the peace as soon as it was won. Many of them are still busy with us. The threat of invasion, which had looked as black as Doomsday, has passed. Now war workers and others, able to breathe freely, have a chance to reflect in the wearying and anxious fifth year of it. They are considering a little of history. This history is so recent that it has been an experience of most of the men in the fighting forces. And the conclusion to which many of them have come is simply that this war will be lost if commonwealth is allowed to remain a rhetorical flourish in exhortations before battle.

I should call that good news. It is creative understanding but recently gained. It is a virtue latent in society. Nobody knows what will come of it, but something will come of it.

We are also aware that the release of this power, one way or another, is in the hands of Winston Churchill. He is the national figure who has our destiny in his charge as surely now as in the days of Dunkirk. He is a leader in war who was at once unanimously acclaimed by the British. In extremity, his voice was known, for it sounded from the hearts of the people. It was our fortune to have a great person to express us.

Yet we are still perplexed by the fact that, having been given the glad franchise of the folk, he should afterwards have accepted as a crowning honour the headship of the party group which had rejected him a few months before the explosions began, and was largely responsible for the inauspicious conditions in which we entered battle. This may mean no more, of course, than that he is a magnanimous man, as well as a leader of courage, fidelity, and vision, whose quickening spirit did most to avert catastrophe. Though we feel this certainty, we shall never free ourselves from the distrust brought about long ago by a famous Business Government. That must be reckoned with as are the fatal rocks marked conspicuously in a mariner's chart.

We maintain the hope, however, that our leader is affected not only by our gratitude, which will not fail, but by a personal intuition that human memory is not always so shallow as some of his important associates may desire it to be. It is very certain that if the British could find it in them to face Hitler when he was triumphant and they had no help, they will have no fear, should further conflict be forced on them, of those influences at home now recovering heart since they see they may continue to use their counting-houses without seeking leave of Berlin.

I doubt that Winston Churchill would look upon the confines and outlook of a counting-house as a makeshift for the kind of stately pleasure dome that Kubla Khan decreed. He has never lent his name to the counting-houses, or sought fame there, though he could easily have found it. We are not quite certain that he knows enough of modern economics to be fully aware of the meaning of those international cartels which have turned the old hard choice between socialism and private enterprise into moonshine. He is not acquisitive, and perhaps fails in full sympathy for men who are. He paints when at leisure, and is satisfied with a job or two about the house and garden.

These simple preferences are always of importance when we have to judge how a man may consider a supplication. But once out in the open, with a purpose, he is just as bold and imaginative an adventurer as an Elizabethan, as Sidney or Raleigh. When he was young, there being no lands to discover in uncharted seas, no Low Countries or Spanish Main, and no dangerous intrigues in the court of an unmarried, exacting, and subtle queen of genius, he took to electoral contests; a poor substitute, but all he could get. Let it be said that they were sufficiently exciting, for the franchise then was wide, and revolt against an old dispensation was already bold; indeed, politics were ruder and fiercer then than now.

He fought his elections always in happy abandon of what his party wanted him to do, and usually he won. He prefers danger in circumstance, and makes it if it is not already there. After the Boer War, which was fairly brief, with no other similar entertainment in prospect, nothing was left for him but the clangor and dust of party politics. And they were tumultuous enough for even a reckless adventurer. Dublin and Belfast could provide a fury of irrational purpose.

Sidney and Raleigh were soldiers who were also men of letters in the charitable tradition, as was usual with courtly

Elizabethan adventurers. Churchill is like them in that. We may doubt that he finds some modern books, praised in select intellectual circles, and said to show a signal advance in apprehension, much to his mind. He may have read them, wondered briefly and simply why the critics were awed, and then, as easement for the labour of the day, turned to the Bible— the Old Testament, naturally—to find words prognostic of the morrow. We may suppose, however, that St. Paul had a manner with backsliders, the false, and the weak-kneed, that Churchill would find of comfort. Those epistles, written to further a cause new and good, have the right fructifying and expanding qualities, and show the way English prose should move when addressed to a high purpose.

Yet a grave and stately parade of words never endears a man to the multitude. Royal purple is admired from a distance. It is not homespun. Our Premier, therefore, is apt to pause, in the midst of his eloquence, when the comic spirit takes him. Humour, being thrifty of words, concludes the matter with a laugh. These inconsequential flashes do more than keep an audience expectant; they reveal a fellow-mortal. A turn of fun shows not only balance, but an understanding of the variety of life in its infinity. While we were still watching for barge-loads of German troops and tanks to nose up our beaches, I remember a broadcast speech of his which at one point gave some of his listeners at home a chill, and then grim amusement. He had reminded us of what we must expect, and it was nothing for comfort, and then suddenly addressed a few words to Hitler: "We are still waiting for that invasion—and so are the fishes."

If it is supposed that the command and resonance of his war speeches and writings are his best accomplishment, and you turn to his work on Marlborough, you meet Sarah, the duke's wife. When she enters the narrative she takes your attention. She is a character, and possessive, and you are glad to see her come into the story again after the pages have been long occupied by bivouacs and battle lines. Evidently the chronicler of Marlborough enjoys the play of a generous and wayward spirit in homely affairs as much as the spectacle of regiments moving through smoke to a decisive event that never, somehow, gives us the decision for which we strive. Humanity and its destiny engage him more, I think, than all the laws and the precedents.

I don't suppose that sense of kinship would have helped us greatly but for this war. He would not clearly have seen what to do. Like the Elizabethans, he must act as well as write, or he is baffled. Movement unites his diverse gifts. And where was choice for action in a fenced and parcelled earth? Even his own party in Parliament feared his reserve of force, and kept him out of office. He might never have risen to his mark but for the astonishment and indignation the eruption of Germany roused in him.

That was his release. He was alarmed. The menace to the best traditional motives for human effort restored to him his youth. Nations were breaking, and their accustomed standards and landmarks, as old as history, were disappearing while men stood dismayed. The bonds of humanity were going, for law and good faith were losing hold in an insurrection of the uncouth and malevolent. Governments were usurped by armed bullies, and no rescue was possible without leaders of vision and energy with a simple faith in the intrinsic kindness of hapless humanity. There it was once more, most unbelievably, a world open for adventure, discovery, and settlement.

Martial triumph would be empty now, unless it were but the prelude. It could not justify its cost in life and labour. Our ac-

customed world has gone. That is the outstanding fact of our
day, and we are beginning dimly to make it out. To understand all it implies will test the quality of our knowledge, and
the worth of our souls. (Shall we mention the forgotten soul
again? We need not be ashamed of it.) We see our earth even
darker than it was when the early navigators were barely
aware of a western continent. It is darker because, while we
are proud to know nearly as much as Lucifer knew—and he
was arrogant through knowledge, so the legend goes—before
he came an awful drop, it gives us no more aid than about
enough to get us through this perilous pass. And then? Then
we shall be in the open, with corruptive wreckage to be cleared,
and communities to be re-established, we are not sure how.
We only know that in all the vast library of political and social
science there is not enough light to show where we are, as we
seek a lasting base for a new society.

What do the ruin and sorrow about us mean except that,
whatever else informed our activities in the past, it was not
the common sense of kindliness? May it now be supposed that
the advice to do to others as we would have them do to us
may have something in it, and be worth trying, after all? Certainly our old equipment for this new adventure, which may
prove man's final effort to get nearer a true course, is inadequate. We feel that. The aids used by explorers in the past to
learn their whereabouts, to fix their position and set a course
into the unknown, cannot help us.

The kingdom we would find has no geographical marks. It
is not described in books, and is unknown in those vast regions
of influence apportioned among industrial monarchs in their
secret designs for controlling us. It is useless to seek it in
this august authority or that. We cannot leave the discovery
of it to our leaders. It is not here, and not there. We can

only look within. It is surprising that this should be found at all strange in a society defending its Christian principles. Do we not see yet that our society is perishing because of its heartless knowledge? And not understand, in this hour, the reason for renunciation?

Each of us must choose, and stand by his choice at all hazards. What choice will Winston Churchill make? His responsibility, when this passage is made, will be graver than ever before rested on an English Prime Minister. Nothing like it has happened before in our history. We cannot believe he will attempt to turn our faces backward. It would be better for London to remain desolate, if we are to go back to the social muddle, inequity, and cruelty, that ultimately were the cause of this world revolution.

The inquiring spirit of man, and his peaceful possession of the gifts of sun and earth, and that need he feels in rare moments to learn of an origin and purpose never yet revealed, are of first importance. Unless these are secured, the rest turns to ashes. The speed, output, and profit of numberless revolving wheels, and of oil, iron and coal, and uncounted ships, and of ever-increasing cities, are not comparable. They come afterward, when the choice is made, of life or death.

The critics and philosophers are still trying to confuse us over the distinction between the dream and the business, between the romantic and the real—as if reality did not transcend the most extravagant fancies of the fabulists; and but for that I should call Churchill a romanticist. He wonders over the mystery of existence. If a traveller finds himself in the Parthenon as the sun sets, or happens all unexpectant into Toledo Cathedral, he knows in a moment there is something in the striving of man which has never yet found full release in poetry or art, though now and again it sounds in music

like a brief escape of harmony from a world not this. And so
Churchill, in a way now old-fashioned, has made his humble
submission to the suggestions and the values the masters have
learned from Greece and Palestine. Art, we have been assured by some recent intellectual advisers, should be amoral;
at its best it should be without human attributes. But it is
wasting time to turn to the amoral for light on our affairs.
Anyhow, we have had enough of inhumanity. As for economics, what has morality, we are asked severely, to do with
that department of science? I myself think that economics
without morality is the east wind for empty bellies, and a
cause of dry rot in good juicy brains.

Should evidence for this be needed, we have only to look
around. There is the daily newspaper to read. We see at a
glance that political economy cannot be kept out of the headlines, and so it must occasion emotional response. Daily in
antiphon these headlines cry out in hatred of communism or
in praise of communion. It may be mentioned, therefore, that
this fierce debate is nothing new. It was not occasioned by
Russia. It is as old as the difference between rich and poor,
and between fair play and foul. There is no compulsion on a
student to begin with Marx.

The English tradition in the humanities is at least as old
as *Utopia*, which was first published in Louvain in 1516, under
the editorship of Erasmus, a friend of Sir Thomas More. That
wise and witty book, unique in the library of political science
because to read it is a pleasure, ought to be in the hands of all
who have authority over our ways. Dean Swift, whose virility
is never questioned, once called the noble, gentle, and cou-
rageous author of *Utopia* "the person of the greatest virtue
that this age has ever produced." A word which is now scaring
timid people everywhere had no terror for Sir Thomas,

who, however, had the heart to oppose his lusty monarch, Henry VIII, with the usual result. The word pictured for him not a reign of terror, but of peace. Though it makes us nervous, the word has its origin in no more than the idea of mutual trust. It was understood by Adam and Eve. It did not scatter the early Christians, but held them in a brotherhood which withstood the Roman Empire. By what are we alarmed?

It is men and women that matter, and their welfare, first and always. Fellowship is above possessions, and transcends frontiers. We cannot doubt that Churchill has read *Utopia*, and it would be improper to suggest that he regards that masterpiece as no more than the origin of an epithet to dismiss a dream of impossible good. The New Testament could be dismissed for the same reason, and the churches all shut, or else turned into unfrequented museums where useless but curious sermons from mounts and elsewhere could be preserved from worms and dust under glass.

How shall we choose? Nobody clearly knows yet, in Washington, Moscow, or London. That is why miners and others are restless, and young soldiers write home puzzled over so queer a matter as the Allied Military Government of Occupied Territories, asking what it means, and whether or not they are to overcome or establish Fascism. Is it right for generals and admirals to be politicians, they ask, but not privates and sailors? So it is not surprising that the Russians can match our doubts of Moscow with a dry thought or two about us.

When I met those two American friends in London of late, who were eager to learn how things are with us, these indirections and hesitations were about all I could pass on. I discovered, while with them, that my chief concern was to assure them that when the English show uneasiness over Americans it is because we are aware that, without their authority and good will, what ought to be done cannot be done. After victory, if each of the victorious powers should seek its own, we shall have but an uneasy leisure to count our losses, suspect all other men, and wait for the next war while air-transport corporations quarrel over rights, claims, and privileges. It is not an enjoyable prospect. It would be but waiting in the dark, listening for the drone of oncoming bombers.

They are the reasons, though there are others, why a Londoner cannot by daylight find his accustomed city. By day the capital is provisional. The opinions of his neighbours are eddying and veering. Only at night, in loneliness, does his place reappear. It is the abode again of thought and memory. It is populous with ghosts. Affection, driven in by the loud demands, and by the sights and sounds of war, comes out in the twilight with the shadows of what is immemorial and dedicated.

London's streets, after the hour of blackout, are of the past, but continue on as ever to what youth may achieve where all is unnamed and unformed. All good things are possible. It is not dark. The stars are out; for again at night over London, after years of absence, the stars have come back to look at us. They are no longer put out by the lower bold glare of our activities, which are, after all, more inscrutable, more terrifying, than the faint glimmer of the Pleiades. Reality and the heavens are nearer to us at night. Assurance returns in loneliness, and it gives the news of the hour the importance already of scattered relics that have but small relation to what is for the future, latent in the quality of our fellows. Have we not ourselves witnessed the heights to which our youth can rise? Who would dare attempt to limit the virtue in that?

From an outlook in central London in the hour when, dark and brooding, the city is waiting silently for the next call in war, for the searchlights to go up and the guns to shake us, there our own place is again. We have it still. Its black parapets and towers are uplifted among the constellations, one with eternity. It is a strangely beautiful London to a watcher whose duty is on the ramparts at night, as mysterious as a city of Eastern fable. Old Samarkand was like this. It is antiquity in continuity. You might think it irrevocably set in the past, remote from a new day; but, looking out over it the other night, trying to get my bearings, I could not find the star I sought. At that point over there it should have been, and at that moment. Was I mistaken in my outlook, or had a star failed me? Yet as I watched, quite still, puzzled and uncertain of myself, doubting the very aspect of the heavens, there suddenly the bright star was. It was only behind a chimney. The earth was shouldering into the east. We were on our way.

IX

New Horizon

MARCH 1944. Because I was at sea in the days of sail—a poor recommendation—I have been allowed to read, though bound to secrecy, the war logs of a fleet of merchant ships. The logs were laconic, of course, as is proper with the professional observations of craftsmen, and too often they alluded to technical matters not easily interpreted. But, after all, a tanker would be a ship to puzzle Nelson, who might not think its destruction by an alliance of submarine and airplane altogether gentlemanly.

In truth, what I read in those logs from all oceans was so peculiar and grisly, and was accepted by the sufferers so casually, as though extinction by the shipload, and fantastically, was only what men should expect, as were the accidents in ancient fables when the gods were jealous and men were new to the earth, that I saw we were indeed in another era, and that it had the augury of a frightful dream. My days of the sailing-ship, though fairly recent, are with Columbus.

I resolved in the first shock of this surprise that some day, and the sooner the better, landsmen, who are most of us, must be told of it. It had become necessary to acknowledge, with due humility in repentance, the nature of the new world that has been created since the spirit of God moved upon the face of the waters and there was light. Darkness once again is upon the face of the deep. But a time comes, and we may be in it, when horror sinks into apathy. Starved men and women shambling out of prison camps, or crawling from under a home crumbled by a bomb, or falling from a cloud in flames, are not interested in ships torn asunder. People, if released on probation from purgatory, do not look back at the prospect from which, temporally, they are free. They want ease of heart, if it can be got.

What writer could heighten, for general reading, with significance enough, those technical reports by seamen too weary to notice the fact that they still exist? When ugliness is the daily aspect of sunrise, what is there for a poet to sing about? No benefit could come of lifting the eyes to the hills.

Do we understand that that is where we are? Must we end with loose hands, and minds surrendered, through apathy? We had better speak plainly to each other while there is time for it, before the soul dies out utterly, though we grow cleverer and more energetic than ever. When the things we do would make Belial mute, the threat of hell is superfluous, for there we are.

I was reading a story recently by a municipal engineer. It was his first attempt at a relation of events, his usual duty being the water, light, power, roads, and drains of a city. His interest was science. He solved problems mathematically. If the marvels of the human spirit are not subject to a slide rule, and they are not, why should a busy man waste time on them? It was enough to preserve the health of these people. You cannot provide for the unpredictable.

His city was Singapore. There, all had been lawful and established for so long that the disturbing whispers of Japanese self-interest on the prowl were confined to the clubs; they circulated after dark. But one day this engineer heard Japanese guns. The next day his work was all for the succour of a huge and variegated population which had not provided against the sky falling on them. Somewhat later, ordered to go, he gave his automobile to an embarrassed soldier who was passing, and boarded a ship bound for he did not know where, and neither did her captain. In his story, soon after that, this passage occurs:

"As St. Valentine's Day, 1942, was nearing its close, a state of affairs which defies description prevailed in this section of the Malay Archipelago. Perhaps never before in the long period of recorded history was there anything to compare with it. Men, women, and children, in ones and twos, in dozens, in scores, and in hundreds, were cast upon these tropical islands within an area of say four hundred square miles. Men and women of many races, of all professions, engineers, doctors, lawyers, business men, sisters, nurses, housewives, sailors, soldiers, and airmen, all shipwrecked. Between the islands on the phosphorescent sea floated boats and rafts laden with people; and here and there, upheld by his lifebelt, a lone swimmer was striving to make land. All around the rafts and lifeboats were dismembered limbs, dead fish, and wreckage drifting with the currents; below, in all probability, were sharks; and above, at intervals, the winged machines of death. Among those who had escaped from death by bombs or the sea was not one who did not suffer from mutilations, wounds, sickness, hunger, cold, dirt, fear, or loss, and none knew what the morrow would bring forth."

That passage is from *Singapore to Freedom,* by Mr. O. W. Gilmour. The picture is of foundations collapsed, establishment gone, society adrift, its symbols of wealth as empty as the signs on an Assyrian brick, of gentle people glad of grasping any flotsam between the devil and the deep. Then were the foundations of society false? I think they must have been. But, whatever the reason may be, we do get a fleeting glimpse of the world as it is, because that picture from the tropics is a common prospect today in all latitudes. The streets of London have often witnessed something like it.

Whether or not the foundations of ordered life have given way, there is nothing false in the way ordinary men and women have faced downfall. That is the heartening thing in this war, and our only hope. It is clear that life has a heroic principle. Between the devil and the deep, that fact floats along to our advantage. Mr. Gilmour was impressed by it; it surprises him at every turn. He noticed the charity of Malays and Chinese to castaways; when they saw distress they forgot their own peril. In young British officers stripped of uniforms and authority there was humour and integrity which catastrophe could not break. No claims were made to property. The man next to you gave away his coat if you were bare; tropical nights can be perishing. Nurses, half-naked on a desert beach, did what they could for the wounded as if a hospital ward were about them.

It was the same in London. There, as in Chungking and Leningrad, people in the street, who left no name behind them, would run to tasks so unprovided for and appalling that the famous heroes of the legends may be forgotten in the name of Anybody. A hero is not distinguished by a badge, he does not look like Roland, but as a rule he is there when wanted. It is true there is a greater "news value" in black markets and other evidence of the residual brute, but it is also true that our modest neighbour has more good in him than we suspected, though he thinks nothing of it, and neither do the newspapers.

This does not mean that he is not a fool, if we measure him by the standard for bright success. It is possible, we are beginning to see, that the standards by which we have valued things hitherto have been short. If a man is only reckoned as a unit of industrial energy, then he is lost in statistics. We do not know he is there. We ask of a cog in a mechanical system only that it should be a sound cog. We talk of humanity, but that is only an abstraction; humanitarians waste affection on a myth. There are persons, and they feel it when hurt. This strikes us as extraordinary only because we have been thinking, in a mechanical age, of our neighbours as manpower.

The standards in common use make it easier for us to account now for the collapse of our order. Had we known how to judge values, had we known no more than the right way to define success, we might have stared at Vanity Fair, and merely wondered how long it could last. We recall today that not a few observers had for years been warning us that we were on a steep place, that we were going too fast, and that the sea was below. Even now it is not easy to reduce to a prime motive our old way of living, unless it were no more than to buy in the cheapest and sell in the dearest market; and that does not seem sufficient to secure acquittal from a rigorous judge. It was unreasonable of society to sharpen the instinct to possess, as the test of a fellow, and then expect the best of him. Our enemies are teaching us to what that instinct leads, when every restraint goes and it rises to the passion and argument of religion, with a believing nation behind it, fully armed.

When nations scattered and were lost, what held us from going with the rest was none of the national institutions which exact obedience, or at least draw some puzzled attention, the

Church, Parliament, Congress, the Bank of England, Wall Street, monarchy or republicanism, or whatever else of the State has been above rude question. It was none of these, nor all of them together. It was the common person. His feeling, when he heard the challenge, was the response in the body of the people. There was no doubt, and no argument. There was an uprising. It was prevalent virtue in revolt from malevolence.

Not by chance does it happen that the root meaning of virtue is man. It is a curious fact that though his energy is spent in trying to win enough bread, with but brief time to consider existence, yet at a word he will break life habits and every law of political economy. He rarely owns enough to make a fight over it worth while, but he has a latent quality, otherwise useless, which treachery is likely to provoke, and in a day the common person is as high as Olympus, with for liars the same threat of thunderbolts about a stormy head.

That seems incredible in an age of scientific materialism, when we can unlock the forces of nature, for any purpose we choose, but see in the soul of man no natural value that would increase the potency of our devices for control; nevertheless, there it is. Reason and evidence are transcended. Physical experiments cannot explain it. The cynicism of realists is silenced; or it is until the valour of the humble has shaped another reality, in which cynics may feel safe and comfortable again. Isn't it enough to make one believe that there exists, as the discarded humanists used to tell us, a power of the spirit, and that miracles are nothing much?

As stories of mysteries are said to be popular, I should say that something near the ultimate mystery is there, and that to get light on it would take a longish book; either that, or a parable. But who would write it? And who would believe?

Science has found no way to release this secret of human life to our advantage, though word of it is in the earliest scriptures and songs, and has survived the wars and squalor of millennia. When we are grieved by old and new horrors, and are reminded pessimistically that humanity never changes, we should remember also that neither does this principle change, despite neglect, persecution, and the blind trampling of never-ending droves of beasts. It is perennial, like the flowers of the field. It has their original resource. It is as certain as the demonstrations of mathematics. It can be read in the eyes of a child, felt in a poem, heard in music, and seen in the face of a man who somehow knows that this will be his last operational flight. Though it is absent from the market-place, it would as well repay our wonder as whatever overcomes thought in the outer gulfs of the night sky. I think it must have a meaning of greater importance to us than anything else that engages us. Unless we learn more of its purport, how remote will be triumph!

The chances and entanglements of sensational fiction, and the airing of scandals in the press, after this affair is past, should have the attraction for us of yesterday's bus tickets. We know now that a situation cannot form, unprecedented and terrible, but somebody there will go to face it. No grotesque invention could match the hesitating yarn of the fellow next to you in a London bus. You find he is a Pole, and that he has just emerged from the darkness of Central Europe. As he talks of his experience, without emotion—you are more shocked than he is, apparently—Trafalgar Square ahead looks spectral.

One meets boys who have made voyages and come through hazards a relation of which would check Odysseus at his fables; but we shall not get those yarns; all will dissolve in the universal nightmare. What excitement is in the clashes of the

Iliad for the pilot who has spent five minutes over Berlin in a plane on fire, two engines stopped, and who must chance it again next week? A passer-by in a London street, one night, entered a house to get a woman out of bed while there was time. Her bed was in the basement, water was rising from a burst main, and what of the house was not already down was blazing. He burrowed through rubble, and dived to ease the twisted iron of the bedstead. The woman was held fast. When the flood nearly filled the room he had to give up, and swam about in the dark to find the place of his entry, but it had gone. A fall of burning rafters presently made a gap and a glare, and he got out.

Should we recommend Ambrose Bierce to that man? I see no good in it, nor would thousands more who have listened to explosions for hours, waiting their turn. We have discovered that reality can be illusory, and its shapes not to be trusted, as might be expected when revolutionary opinions are at work; but we can at least see to it that sanity is kept at the centre. What shall we want of imagined incoherence and manias after this year?

For some time in this war I saved instances of good work done where good, in the situations reported, must have seemed no good at all. Still, somebody there proved superior to the impossible, and brought good about. It was not long before the collection was so large that I could see I was only keeping an unnecessary account of a man we all know. Nothing was extraordinary in it, except ignorance of the fact that this was his character. Though humanity never changes, neither does he. He might be a favourite of the elements, and immune. From the ice age of prehistory to the disasters recorded today he comes out, rather dazed, to begin again upon another home. All the never-ending blunders of statecraft have done nothing to reduce his faith and hope; and that is astonishing in a backward glance, for by now he should be extinct.

Yet he has survived every great work on his behalf by princes and men of action. Whatever happens to him, there comes a nudge from his forgotten past, and out he goes to prove superior to calamity. The story that he responds only to the drive of self-interest is now foolish. The impossible has been done. It is accomplished daily, and not by economists, lawyers, and politicians, nor by experts so well informed that they cannot take a first step, but by the man of no importance. He is doing the impossible for no better reason than that he sees no other choice. He fails at times, we know, and not seldom; but his own sort following after him take up the task and the lesson.

The other day in London the streets were thick and brisk with the martial uniforms of many nations. I saw the orris of a score of captains and several admirals in five minutes west of Charing Cross. But to meet, as I did, a man with whom I had talked in the navigation room of his ship during the middle watch, long ago, was rather like running into the past, and recognizing a shade. He really is a sailor, and a master mariner, though dressed as he was one might not have guessed it; not a trace of gold lace, but he spent ten years under sail. He was no more conspicuous that day than any other elderly nobody; though if only he would write the story of his life afloat it would make the fabulists see they are thrifty of excitement. But he will never write it. To suggest it to him would only make him ribald.

Eyeing a group of soldiers, he mentioned casually that the likes of him were being asked to volunteer for service at a second front, wherever that was likely to be. I did not ask him whether he had booked for it. There was no doubt he had.

Sailors will sign-on for whatever is going. They know nothing of heroism, but trust to luck. For my friend, a voyage to the shores of that legendary front will be only another voyage. He has not been surprised since he was an apprentice. He had a long winter voyage in an open boat in the last war. He had his boats out of the davits again in a London dock this war, and in tow for Dunkirk. It was at short call, and it must have been a voyage and a half, but all he says of it is, "Well, we had fair weather for it." Most of his stories are of the comic sort. He rejects publicity as unpleasant. But if ever you hear with deep distaste great seas running at night, when your ship is foundering, he is the man to have near you; but then, if that mischance comes, you will find such a sailor near you, most likely, though you may not know his name.

A retired admiral, who returned to service as a commodore of convoys, confessed some months ago—since his word with us on the humours of directing convoys he has joined the missing—that when he first went to sea with them he doubted the ability of a great number of merchant seamen to act in concert as would navy men. Keep station? Why, with ships of various sizes, ages, design, and speed? He had little hope. He was doubtful of himself. How command that assembly, should it be hunted? He interviewed phlegmatic bowler-hatted men, who had no advice to give him. He told them what he wanted, but wondered, privately, how seamen could do it, and keep it up, with such vessels, and weather on its way to meet them. He judged it better, when at sea, not to worry these untried strangers with anxious signals, and so left his charges, blacked out in a storm, to Providence.

One sunrise, the seas immense and the wind still high, he looked round for his flock, expecting the worst. But there it was, despite its limitations, in pretty good array, as to the

manner born. When attacked at last it held its course as if
nothing under heaven could make it change its gait. It could
go on like this while it floated. He had an idea these merchant-
men-at-arms rate the shocks of war, torpedoes, bombing, and
gunfire, as hardly comparable with their customary hazards,
fog, blizzard, hurricane, collision, and poor food and low pay.
He didn't believe anything could happen at sea to which they
would not try to adjust themselves, and perhaps succeed, as
men used to all the variations of hard luck.

When the convoy makes the land, war has not done with it.
A central bureau must disperse it, and direct each ship to
where its cargo had better be discharged, as things stand then;
and circumstance can be altered out of recognition, and in a
brief time, through the anarchy of battle. The shipowner and
his private interest, moving his tonnage to his judgment of
markets and facilities, is in abeyance. A body of maritime
students, who have privy knowledge, dispose of tonnage as the
needs of the commonweal and its armies require.

This management of ship and freights used to be regarded
as an unachievable dispensation, the certain way to national
ruin; but it works. It works miraculously well. Private enterprise, faced with the task of serving the national interest un-
conditionally, is short in mental equipment. Such a revolutionary demand changes the world before its eyes into one it
does not know and cannot understand. As with the man who
once was curious about the way to salvation, private interest
must be born again; and in war there is no time for that; a
new birth might take too long and come too late.

Then a pilot takes over a ship. He also is anonymous. The
year when charts and experience told him what to do is past.
Since last he guided a ship into that harbour, perhaps the
night before, its landmarks, mine-fields, soundings, buoys, and

sandbars may have been reassorted. A shower of bombs can transform even a faithful fairway. It will look as aforetime, but the set of currents are not what they were, and yesterday's safe lead is a peril today to be avoided by prayer, while making calculations which a pilot hopes will suit his ship's draught.

The ability in the common person to meet with steady patience, and no resentment, life in a new aspect is revealed only when a community is in peril. We had forgotten what a long experience with trouble that man has had since he first made a fire and pushed out a coracle. He can face anything, even new social arrangements designed for his good. Clearly we may depend on him, at least, if our present intent to direct human affairs to a better purpose after this is honestly felt. But he himself may have something to say about that, and he is most of the folk.

Two friends from Boston—one the editor of the *Atlantic Monthly*—stood with me on London ground once familiar to me, but that day scarcely to be made out. Explosions had riven it, fire had gone through it. Miracles of modern inventions had been worked upon it. It was a London dock, known to readers of *The Mirror of the Sea,* and to me since childhood. The dockmaster saw us and asked our business, but was reassured. His jacket, showing the rank of naval commander, was well decorated for service in other wars. We liked the look of him, and he must have been sure of us, for he became communicative, dryly. We looked round that rectangular basin, out of which, we were told, ships had been warped on a September night that appeared to be London's end, and expressed surprise. What, big ships shifted? In that limited space hurriedly? At night? "We had plenty of light," was all he said.

For my part, I felt that more than a familiar scene had gone. The past was with it, blotted out. We stood where, till lately, an old tradition, and the names of the men who had made it, and a way of life first instituted by companies of merchant adventurers nearly three centuries ago, were still of the daily life of a London parish. But the day the three of us saw it, it was jagged walls and rubble and nondescript relics of the past, waiting for resurrection to sound; though all was quiet when we left it. No trumpet yet.

That dockmaster had plenty of light. But what a light! As if all we had laboured to get went up lurid as Hades itself, once the elements of existence were at an unlucky juncture and were touched off. In so revealing a light we could see, and not for the first time, that we had not gained on the original hairy savage as much as we had supposed. There is no essential difference between a flint arrow-head and an aerial bomb. They are aimed by the same thought. The whole of our elaborate system for social well-being, with its power-stations, banks, and aerodromes, its doles, bread lines, and funeral expenses guaranteed by legislatures, turns into an offensive smell with a change of wind and an idiot's dab of phosphorus. What is this conquest of nature we boast about? It begins to look very much like the suicide of mankind.

Frankenstein's monster goes over our communities with their treasuries of the best that man has done, and leaves them foul heaps of ash and bones. Well, was it supposed that our common way of life, not much affected by the Church and all, in which the devil was welcome to the hindmost, could be made holy, in lieu of a god, by magic out of a physical research station? No more than that seems to have been our faith. This very day, despite all warning lessons, we show our mental preferences as disdainfully and ruinously as ever. A tolerance of ugliness in a nihilistic age is to be expected, and gives our daily prospect. If beauty is not functional, to use a cant word, it can be discarded with the rest of the outworn. It is forgotten that only in a humble awareness of the past, with its errors and triumphs, and a sensitiveness to high values, and a rendering to material power of not a jot more than belongs to it, is our hope for the future.

So we close down the Humanities even at the universities. How significant that is! Do not the Nazis, as a matter of duty, burn libraries?—which is only a bit further along the same road. The arts today are shut to youth. Students are exempt from battle only if their studies are directed to perfection in the science of destruction. And nobody worries about this; nobody, that is, to whom a legislature need give more attention than it ever gives to the signs of the times. "A thing of ugliness," says Sir Arthur Helps, "is potent for evil. It deforms the taste of the thoughtless; it frets the man who knows how bad it is; it is a disgrace to the people who raise it— an example and an occasion for more monstrosities."

We have reason for a new song of praise, then, since we have found that the heart of the common man transcends the devices of statecraft and the mockery of the cynics. His virtue, free at the call, is of proved greater value and potency than whatever further power science can discover and release. We could at least depend on him not to go on mutilating our tender planet, for gain, till it is a dead star.

X

Christmas Eve

DECEMBER 1941. "Is there anybody there?" cried the Traveller in the poem, before the house. It was silent. In the twilight the old abode appeared abandoned, and voiceless but for echoes. But we travellers in time will continue to question the reserve of the past. Surely we are heard. Our ancient house must have memory. Oblivion would be contempt. Where birth and death have been, where men have laughed and grieved, can no impression remain? Walls must be haunted. The earth does not forget?

For doubt is sure to take us as we appeal. It was pride in the Traveller that forced the cry from him. He knew he had some worth. He was human and lonely, and desired communion and the assurance of continuity. Was it possible he was unremembered and deprived? Fear took him with the thought that from a place that is desolate memory also has passed; that in all a man has felt and thought and done there is no ultimate importance.

Personal memory can be so acute. That sensitiveness may mislead us. A mere trace of the past is indelible by the heaviest of events. And looking back, a long life will seem all as memorable as but an evening gone. Is that backward glance without purport, though its vista suggests abundance and perenniality? Yet we are aware of the grim fact that those hours of a long life, relatively, are but as a tick of the clock. Going back past most human records, where, we ponder, is

the memory, except for the lucky fragment of a fresco, of the
three ladies in blue who used to know their way about the
lost city of Knossos? That survival of a mural tells us they
were once as delicately aware of things as the brightest of us.
They were vivacious and lovely girls, but that was before the
Iliad was written. It was a commonplace to them, the public
spectacle which occasioned a silly story of a minotaur in a
labyrinth. They knew the truth about it. When they danced
there must have been emotion and cries where now are silence
and innominate stones. Who remembers? We would give
something to be sure their invisible presence is now aware of
another invasion of Crete, once more the barbarians, and that
they watch in amusement the solemn confidence of this new
late lot in jack-boots. Is there anybody there?

We hope so. We want to believe the earth never forgets the
trifles of joy and innocence. Hope is most of our possessions
now, and we must hold on to that while we can. Another poet
has assured us there is no ultimate forgetting; and even while
we wonder doubtfully whether there can be long remembrance for man who suffers in his flesh alone, whether there
are lasting tablets for the appeal driven from his body in conflict with principalities and powers, we cannot help wondering at the same time over the certainty of earth's accurate
recollection of the multitudinous delicate patterns in the lives
of lesser creatures, from the day of their creation. Maybe
nothing is forgotten. We have to turn to the poets for confidence, especially at this season of the year, when we all look
back in appraisal. It is no good turning to science, which
has greater knowledge, because that is too busy on war-time
research to be bothered; all for the future! The only light it
has for the shadows behind us is electric, its thumb on a
predestined switch. Nothing is there, it tells us. And it is true

that most of us, eyes to the past, have never seen a ghost, even when, in the right hour and place, we have invited one. Nor do I expect ever to see one. But my knowledge is next to nothing. I cannot see in the dark; and there are sounds of life's activities that are beyond the range of human hearing.

Once, when at sea, a chance turn of a button of the radio box surprised the cabin with the voice of a friend of mine, talking casually a thousand miles way. Till the moment of that accident with a wave-length I was unaware his voice was sounding, for whoever chose to listen, above the soughing of the billows, where nothing was in sight but the stars. Queer! One who sat listening with me, and he an engineer and a student of what are called natural laws, began to speculate later about that possibility of ultimate remembrance by the circumambient. He reminded me that we had been told to believe that even the fall of a sparrow is marked. "Well, then, if we knew enough, knew the wave-length, might the void release the sound of other voices long silent? Cleopatra's? Nearer our day, wasn't there enough passion in a parsonage at Haworth to make an impression on any sensitive element? Does the earth recall the shouts in the pass of Thermopylae? Could the voices on the Somme be heard again if we knew the way to listen? I wish I knew the way."

Then he smiled, and quoted "Hans Breitmann gife a barty —vhere is dot barty now?" He went below to his engines, leaving me in the alley-way amidships, which was deserted, for the wind was hard, to eye Sirius over Africa, to listen to sounds that were older than time, and to understand that Hans Brietmann's party had as much right to perpetuity for its non-sense as had the spiritual stress in the dark house at Haworth. There could be no distinction made. If one, then the other. The only answer to the sound of midnight seas, where nothing

was in sight but the constellations which guided the Phoe-
nicians when they were about, was to kiss the hand blithely to
it all. Remembrance in reserve of some sort it would be perilous
to deny. One could climb into the bunk, and sleep on so much
of certainty, with the wind ahead, and the seas rising.

It was not a poet but a practical man of affairs who told
us that "our sympathy is cold to the relation of distant misery."
That man would be inattentive—better for his peace of mind
that he was—to plaintive numbers that flow, "for old unhappy
far-off things, and battles long ago." And we may suppose that
to him the remembrance of festivals and foolish and happy
occasions would be sentimental, and a waste of good usable
time. Even for the sentimental, those foolish but happy occasions in the past will hardly bear looking at when we turn,
this year, to the good fortune of Decembers gone. The vitality
and gusto of Dickens himself, exploring London as it is for
another Christmas story, might be inclined to give this number
a miss; not suitable for *Household Words*! The other day,
drawn by the past, I went to a London parish I used to know
well enough; my first Christmas was there, and more to follow.
I had felt at home in that parish with John Company, the
Blackwall frigates and the China clippers. The house-flags of
ships of famous lines topped dock walls, while boys dawdled
on their way to school, recognizing proper emblems aloft. A
man whose ship had been ice-bound in Hudson Bay once told
me all about it, in the very ship, when at long last she docked
with us again. I remember she had outboard channels—we
shall never see the like of that again—for I climbed aboard by
one, though that was not the thing to do. She has gone now,
of course, but that day's sun is still bright on the run of her
deck; and on much else in the parish where she moored.

Something checked me as I neared the old place the other

day. One landmark had gone; and soon I might have been amid the ruins of Ypres. Ypres was like this. I stood in one familiar area and saw nothing alive, except a venerable woman seated on rubbish before a house that had a view clear through it to a wilderness beyond. I was unsure of my whereabouts, for the rubble of downfall covered all landmarks, but I did not dare question that old crone. Her head was in her hands, and her grey hair loose on her shoulders. On a toppled wall behind her a shutter dangled askew to a blind window, and somebody had nailed to it a rescued bedroom text, the only dot of colour amid general ashes. The text counselled acceptance, but I will not quote it. That old woman had accepted, I could see. I thought she might be the wife of Tom of Bedlam.

A house I sought, knowing it well, was not there. It had vanished utterly. All around it had gone. Its very site was lost. We have heard it said of a man that "the places that knew him shall know him no more." Yet if he himself still see daylight and remember, but the familiar places have vanished? How then?

It is very confusing. I could not call out to the house, "Is there anybody there?" Even that was refused. What some of London's ghosts will do now I don't know. There is nowhere for them to go. Marley would be in a fix this year, and Scrooge sleep undisturbed; in an Anderson, perhaps. If any of the ghosts of London are still drifting about, looking for what is not here, then we have a deal of work before us to give them another London which will satisfy their memory of the right good thing and keep them with us.

But they must wait a little. To see things change till at last they are absorbed by time is one thing, but when the landmarks and tokens are obliterated overnight our sense of continuity, which accepts change with fair ease, suffers damage.

The verities topple. Instead of progression is vacuity. So are the foundations few of us have ever questioned but provisional? Then where is secure standing? On what can we build?

Who can tell us? To consider, as an interesting speculation, that reality is what you will, and that all appearance is phantasmal, increases the entertainment of life's adventure as we reach for the decanter again in good company. All's well! Appearance lasts long enough for us. The hills are not eternal; still, they will not vanish while we watch. Even the Bank rate varies so little that it might be controlled by whatever brings about lunar phases. But nowadays you cannot help feeling a little spectral yourself—like the people about you—on a raid night, when the heavens seem to be rolling up. The people in the dugout, which smells of the mould, sit huddled, faintly seen in a vague light, as if waiting for the trumpet's final blast. Then they will go up. Nor is that the worst of it, though we have heard those underground spectres burst into merriment at a jest we did not hear. The worst of it, by far, is the disappearance of old bonds, old associations, and the standards by which we assessed things. Gone! There are no sanctities. They are overturned, and mingled with the brick-bats. It is useless to appeal to the old house. Nobody is there. Its very bounds have vanished with the door-knocker. It is nothing.

Nothing? We are not going to believe that, not with the very fact before our eyes. Though all goes, though nothing remain of what was good but the personal memory of it, we shall have to hold on to that, if as isolated survivors. Somehow the damnable fact shall be proved to be only a misleading appearance. What, is only evil true? Not while two or three rebels against things as they are can form a secret sanctuary of their own, and in communion testify to what light they know. The world of appearance, whatever its formidable arsenals, is no more permanent than the ideas of the common mind from which it is projected. Lift your thought and change your world.

I remember a Christmas Eve when dark and minatory appearance was just what it is now. It was somewhere in the neighbourhood of the Somme. I had gone to that region to find a friend in the line. Certainly there was enough desultory shelling that day, but one noticed it only absently. It could not matter. The earth was dead already, and a wayfarer would merely join it. Life had gone, the trees and grass had gone. What remained was a skin of grey mud which glistened leprously, its putrid surface ghastly with green and reddish pools. The sky was low over it, the colour of the mud, and apparently of the same consistency. There were objects scattered about the scene, but let them be absent from a description of it. My friend, when I parted from him, turned by the corner of a shallow drain, stood there for a moment and held up his hand, smiling, and then was round the corner. I remained at my corner for a moment, looking back, as if he might reappear, but he never did. Nothing moved, except the rag of a sandbag hanging in the wind, which was exposed when he turned away. No midnight stars, for that place. I did not see how even a special star, that eve of Christmas, could get a hopeful beam through to it. In fact, I did not think of such a possibility. All I saw around was the dreary manifestation of the will of mankind as then it was disposed. I turned and trudged back through the solvent and unregenerative muck, with no light, followed by sullen shell-bursts and black eruptions. There could be no change in such a common mind as that, which had chosen to give fertility the appearance of an opened sepulchre. I cursed prevalent opinion, which had sunk my friend in its sea of unnamable filth.

On my way out of it westward I came to a small town. By now it was dusk, and in the public square was a church which, from its porch, seemed to be of the Middle Ages. The buildings of the square had suffered, and the church itself was imperfect. There was time to waste, and I found the church door would give, when I pushed it. I could go in, and did. There was nothing else to do, till a car came for me.

The only light in the church was from the sanctuary; candles there on the floor responded to draughts. Their upward-shaking reflections made the beams and the pillars of the nave illusory, for they also wavered, as if unsubstantial. I was not surprised by this indecision of the old foundation. Thus I felt myself. I was not sure that I dared do more than tiptoe in such a place, for a sound might have shaken it, might have brought it down; as if I had chanced, wide-awake, among the shapes of a dream which betokened a world that was, a world of peace then forgotten. I thought I would keep the good illusion as long as I could, and so tiptoed through it. Not a sound.

On the floor of the sanctuary was the Nativity scene. The candles were lighting that. The puppets were complete to the ass and the ox. They stood respectfully, these toys, before the central figures. There it was illustrated, the legend for Christian children, with even an announcing angel suspended over all by a wire. The angel danced as if in joy through the draught I had let into the church. As I counted by candlelight the little show, making sure all were present, I could hear the melancholy boom of guns, the guns of our endless war.

Then, over against me, I noticed, almost merged in the shadows, three women in black on their knees. In those days all Frenchwomen were in black, but these were old women. They were in obeisance to the scene over which a tinsel angel was still whirling in a dance. The candles began to steady again.

The three women were speaking, for their lips were moving, but I heard nothing. They were not speaking to me. Either they did not see me or I was an irrelevant intruder. And I was irrelevant, I and my thoughts, and the frightful mud on my boots, without doubt. Here survived and was kept the memory of a word once passed to men for their good; and I was frowning over it, trying to recall it, and to adjust it to the reality I knew, if I could. But for some reason, or for no reason—as reason is properly understood—I no longer felt like cursing, even on behalf of my friend. Those kneeling women were in a world not mine; but their world was veritable, for though their speech was unheard it was, I could see, addressed respectfully to whatever had bowed the likes of the humble in reverence for as long as France had known seed-time and harvest. By the look of them they had seen much in this life and had felt all I had known of its stress. After all, what could I add to their knowledge if I broke the quiet? Nothing at all. It was just possible, since the surge of hate had lessened in me, that all of us present could talk of the same things and in much the same way. But I did not try. Knowledge that it could be done was sufficient.

Let them, I thought, keep this little reminder of a lovely story. Whatever we may think of the announcing angel, something did happen, beyond question, which merited a new star of particular splendour for men of good will in all lands to see. A new word was born; by the light of it the greatest artists and poets as well as the saints have since worked. It established an ultimate value by which we judge all.

While I was confessing this to myself there was an ugly burst somewhere near; one more reminder of present reality. The three women did not move. They might not have heard it. Perhaps they knew the memory that was theirs could not be put out by all the guns of all the hosts. It was in perpetuity, unforgotten while sunrise and sunset should last. It must have been such an assurance which kept them so still, for I, too, heard that noise but as a passing mischance.